NATIONAL GEOGRAPHIC

the poetry of US

With favorites from Maya Angelou, Walt Whitman, Gwendolyn Brooks, and more

More than 200
poems that celebrate the
people, places, and *passions*
of the United States

Edited by J. Patrick Lewis, former U.S. Children's Poet Laureate

NATIONAL GEOGRAPHIC
WASHINGTON, D.C.

New England   14

Maine, New Hampshire, Vermont, Massachusetts,
Rhode Island, and Connecticut

Mid-Atlantic   32

New York, Pennsylvania, New Jersey, Delaware,
Maryland, and Washington, D.C.

Southeast   58

Virginia, West Virginia, Kentucky, Tennessee,
North Carolina, South Carolina, Georgia, Alabama,
Mississippi, Arkansas, Louisiana, Florida

Midwest   84

Ohio, Indiana, Michigan, Illinois, Wisconsin,
Minnesota, Iowa, and Missouri

Great Plains 108

North Dakota, South Dakota, Nebraska, Kansas,
Oklahoma, and Texas

Rocky Mountain West 134

Montana, Idaho, Wyoming, Colorado, Utah,
New Mexico, Arizona, Nevada

Pacific Coast 152

California, Hawaii, Oregon, Washington, Alaska

Territories 174

American Samoa, Guam, Northern Mariana Islands,
Puerto Rico, U.S. Virgin Islands

"*All poetry begins with Geography.*"

Robert Frost

J. PATRICK LEWIS HAS WRITTEN MORE THAN 110 PICTURE AND POETRY BOOKS FOR YOUNG READERS. IN 2011 HE WAS APPOINTED U.S. CHILDREN'S POET LAUREATE, AND WAS GIVEN THE NATIONAL COUNCIL OF TEACHERS OF ENGLISH AWARD FOR EXCELLENCE IN POETRY FOR CHILDREN.

YEARS AGO I read a travel book, *Blue Highways*, by a true life wanderer, William Least Heat Moon.

This was no average tour guide, but an epic poem, a love letter to America. In it, the main character drove his green van, called Ghost Dancing, through towns with names like Remote, Bug, Ono, Igo, Badaxe, Lookingglass, Why, and Whynot, discovering the lives and livelihoods, the grit and charm of small-town U.S.A.

Reading *Blue Highways* was like being slapped in the face with a pie—banana cream, my favorite. What unknown wonders had spread themselves across this fine and dappled land without my knowing it. The book made travel easy and cheap. Not the "real" thing, of course, but the armchair variety that could satisfy any kid searching for the experience of otherwhere.

All of which led, circuitously and after a few decades, to the book in your hands, *The Poetry of US*. Here, in chiseled words and fabulous photos from National Geographic's archives, we bring you the underside, backside, inside, and other side of America, the undiluted richness of our national diversity. This book is a cross-country trip across Route 66, or an invigorating hike on the Appalachian Trail. It offers its pleasures vicariously: a backyard barbecue in Idaho, a hog-calling contest in Montana, a garlic festival in California, rituals in a New Mexico sweat lodge, Elvis's Graceland, a drive-in theater, an Amish buggy ride, a swim with a Polar Bear Club, and so many other iconic American destinations.

Transported by this express train of words, you will get a sense of the breadth and depth, the head and the heart, of America. And after you take this journey by book, you might discover, upon getting up from your chair and walking into another room, just where it was you were searching for.

—J. Patrick Lewis,
former U.S. Children's Poet Laureate

America the Beautiful

O beautiful for spacious skies,
For amber waves of grain,
For purple mountain majesties
Above the fruited plain!
America! America!
God shed His grace on thee
And crown thy good with brotherhood
From sea to shining sea!

O beautiful for pilgrim feet,
Whose stern, impassioned stress
A thoroughfare for freedom beat
Across the wilderness!
America! America!
God mend thine every flaw,
Confirm thy soul in self-control,
Thy liberty in law!

O beautiful for heroes proved
In liberating strife,
Who more than self their country loved,
And mercy more than life!
America! America!
May God thy gold refine,
Till all success be nobleness,
And every gain divine!

O beautiful for patriot dream
That sees beyond the years
Thine alabaster cities gleam
Undimmed by human tears!
America! America!
God shed His grace on thee
And crown thy good with brotherhood
From sea to shining sea!

—Katharine Lee Bates

Naming the American Eagle

His flight, it might
  surprise your eyes,
the things his wings
  could dare on air,
the way he'd sway
  then trust each gust
to lift his drifting,
  storming form,
and how his brow
  would wrinkle in
while sporting for
  a meal of eel
the river gives
  to slake his ache
till one more sun
  should set, and yet
the child, she smiled
  and called him bald.

       —Steven Withrow

Our **Rose**

*The national flower of the United States,
the rose is native to almost every state.*

Our rose--our native rose—
opens simple and pink:
a cup of five petals
that offers wild nectar
   for any to drink.

Our rose—our native rose—
grows tender green leaves
and bright scarlet fruit:
a meal for the hungry
   from petal to root.

Our rose—our native rose—
grows thorny and thick:
a tangle of brambles
that shelters the nestling,
   the pup, kit, and chick.

Our rose—our native rose—
doesn't need care or fuss;
just a warm wedge of sunshine,
a sluicing of rain,
   and wild places—
   like us.

—*Joyce Sidman*

The Gift Outright

The land was ours before we were the land's.
She was our land more than a hundred years
Before we were her people. She was ours
In Massachusetts, in Virginia,
But we were England's, still colonials,
Possessing what we still were unpossessed by,
Possessed by what we now no more possessed.
Something we were withholding made us weak
Until we found out that it was ourselves
We were withholding from our land of living,
And forthwith found salvation in surrender.
Such as we were we gave ourselves outright
(The deed of gift was many deeds of war)
To the land vaguely realizing westward,
But still unstoried, artless, unenhanced,
Such as she was, such as she would become.

—Robert Frost

Power to the People: Signs of Our Democracy

(A Found Poem)

I AM A MAN. I AM A MAN.
You Are on Stolen Land.
Your Backwards Views Are Older Than the Dinosaurs.
We Can't Feed the Poor But We Can Fund a War.
Jim Crow Must Go.
End Segregated Rules. Put Prayer Back in Schools.
Stop the H8. The World Can't Wait.
Don't tread on me. Stop Police Brutality. We Demand Equality.
From Adam's Rib to Women's Lib.
Pro-Life. Women's Choice.
Your Vote Is Your Voice.
No More! Outrage! Consumers Crave a Living Wage.
Occupy Wall Street. No More Pollution.
Government Is the Problem, Not the Solution.
Clenched fist. Peace sign. Flying dove.
We are America. Love and Let Love.
Activism is not a crime.
I'm tired of marching for what should already be mine.

—Carole Boston Weatherford

I Hear America Singing

I hear America singing, the varied carols I hear;
Those of mechanics, each one singing his, as it should be, blithe
    and strong;
The carpenter singing his, as he measures his plank or beam,
The mason singing his, as he makes ready for work, or leaves off
    work;
The boatman singing what belongs to him in his boat, the
    deckhand singing on the steamboat deck;
The shoemaker singing as he sits on his bench, the hatter singing
    as he stands;
The wood-cutter's song, the ploughboy's on his way in the
    morning, or at the noon intermission or at sundown;
The delicious singing of the mother, or of the young wife at
    work, or of the girl sewing or washing,
Each singing what belongs to her, and to none else,
The day what belongs to the day—at night, the party of young
    fellows, robust, friendly,
Singing, with open mouths their strong melodious songs.

—Walt Whitman

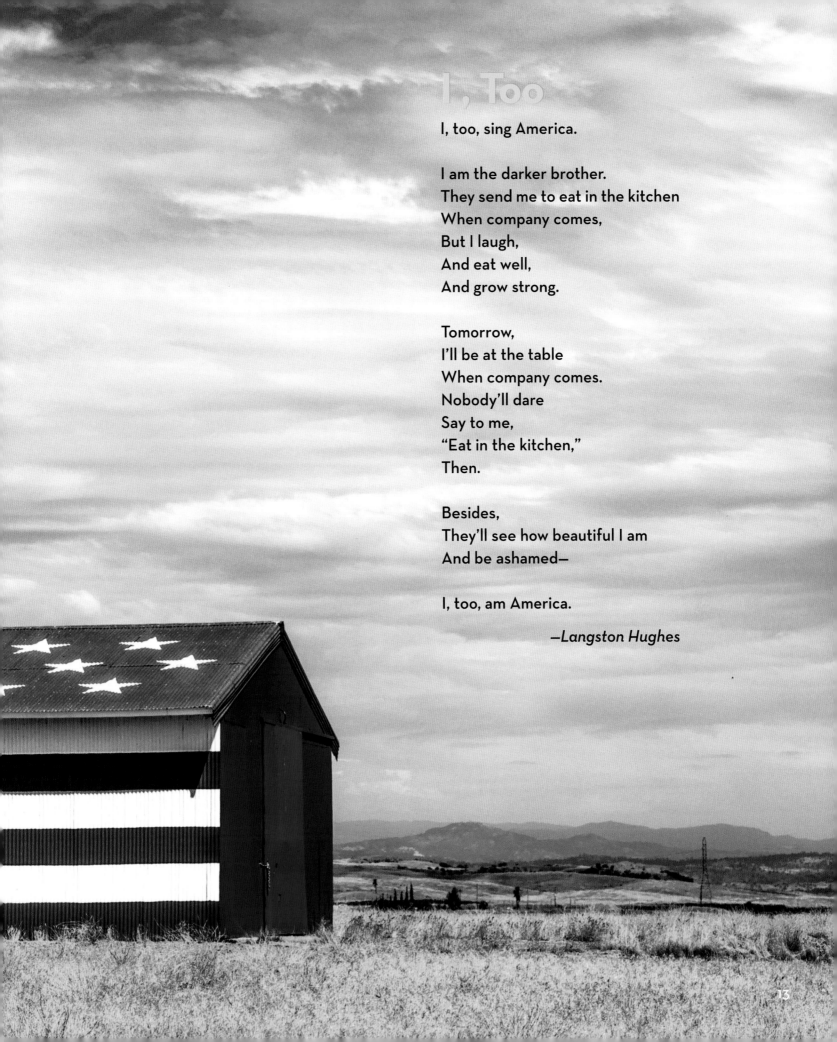

I, Too

I, too, sing America.

I am the darker brother.
They send me to eat in the kitchen
When company comes,
But I laugh,
And eat well,
And grow strong.

Tomorrow,
I'll be at the table
When company comes.
Nobody'll dare
Say to me,
"Eat in the kitchen,"
Then.

Besides,
They'll see how beautiful I am
And be ashamed—

I, too, am America.

—*Langston Hughes*

NEW

ENGLAND

A Note
from the Trail

Through fourteen states I wend my quiet way
yet human borders do not interest me.
I welcome hikers for a year, a day.
I offer gifts of moonrise, birdsong, tree.

All lives are equal when you find them here:
poison ivy, bear, tick, human child.
Old worries dash away like spotted deer.
No bikes, no wheels. Just souls—unfettered, wild.

Each year, three million people run or walk
bits of my two thousand sacred miles.
Some whistle. Some are silent. Others talk.
I celebrate each mountain climbed, each tired smile.

From Maine to Georgia, back and forth I go.
Hike me. Let me change you. Tell the tale.
Learn deep secrets only hikers know.
Welcome. I am the Appalachian Trail.

—*Amy Ludwig VanDerwater*

Spring in New Hampshire

Too green the springing April grass,
Too blue the silver-speckled sky,
For me to linger here, alas,
While happy winds go laughing by,
Wasting the golden hours indoors,
Washing windows and scrubbing floors.

Too wonderful the April night,
Too faintly sweet the first May flowers,
The stars too gloriously bright,
For me to spend the evening hours,
When fields are fresh and streams are leaping,
Wearied, exhausted, dully sleeping.

—Claude McKay

Vermont Seasons

The massive walls of mountains
In the Green Mountain State
Put on new suits of color
Depending on the date,
In fall, wear red and yellow
When maples stage their show,
But soon start in December
To dress up white with snow.

You step through this state's borders,
Start feeling how life slows,
The same way that in springtime
Sweet syrup wakes and flows.
Even the cows don't hurry,
But emulate the trees,
Taking what seems forever
Perfecting cheddar cheese.

"Folks say that your long winter
Is just a thing to dread,
Or else I'd love to live here,"
The summer woman said.
"That's all right," said the farmer.
"We don't mind if you don't.
Shucks, if it weren't for winter
Everybody'd live in Vermont."

—X. J. Kennedy

Whale Watch,
Cape Cod

We counted twenty birds for every whale
Or seal or dolphin rolling at our stern.
Over the sundeck wheeled a fork-tailed tern,
One of hundreds leaving shore. To fail
To see a humpback breach by afternoon,
Afloat in open ocean, may have meant,
To those who were not birders, a day misspent,
For who wouldn't trade a kittiwake or loon,
A gannet or black-backed gull, for forty tons
Of leaping mammal mass? Perhaps a pair
Hoping to spot a petrel in the air
And other long-range migrants. They're the ones
Who watched a white-winged scoter flying out
While, aft, a drifting island blew its spout.

—Steven Withrow

THE INKWELL POLAR BEAR CLUB, BEGUN OVER 70 YEARS AGO, IS A MULTICULTURAL GROUP OF PEOPLE WHO BEGIN THEIR DAY IN THE WATER AT MARTHA'S VINEYARD, MASSACHUSETTS.

Friendship Circle—7:30 AM

They gather early on the sand
For some it's morning prayer
For others exercise
(I've joined them on a dare)
No one asks who you know
Your status, what you do
They only ask your name
So happy that you came
Relax, reflect, renew

And as the tide draws near
(I dip in my big toe)
Ignore the frigid air
The ocean doesn't care
Your age, beliefs or race
The love that fills this place
As everyone joins hands
Is like a warm embrace
I'm now a Polar Bear

—*Richard Michelson*

LUTHER BURBANK
1849-1926

The Man Who Scattered Pollen Underneath the Sun

he wanted only
to feed the world
a better piece of fruit
and more,

a plum that succumbed
to grafted glory,
to oozing perfection
of flavor

a nectarine
that achieved his dream
of pristine texture
and flaming sheen,

a cherry tree
whose season lingered longer
suffused with sweeter juices

and so he took
his tiny seeds
and planted them
and waited,
and when one bore
the best of all,
he shared it

and celebrated

—Michele Krueger

Roadside Farm Stand

There is harmony in tomatoes.
Folks who disagree about taxes
          baseball
          cats vs. dogs
come together over Sungolds and Brandywine Reds,
          sampling and selecting,
          singing the praises of summer's bounty.
Then there's that shared moment of sadness,
everybody knowing it can never last—
     until some cheerful soul says,
          "So enjoy 'em while they're here."
And once again there's a merry band
     always in tune at the roadside stand.

—Marilyn Singer

Blueberry Barrens

Buy a few pints of them
you feel as though
you've struck it rich.

Suddenly it's blueberry everything:
pancakes, pies, tarts and cobblers;
a stampede of berries in your cereal
that stain your teeth dark blue.

They sprout near the coast in low fields
that get burned every other year;
they say ash sparks a sweeter crop.

You stand beside a row of bushes,
nothing special, an ordinary green
until light strikes at just the right angle

and all at once tiny spheres appear,
an intense blue hue,
a field of sapphires
far as the eye can see.

—Ralph Fletcher

Sing Hey-Ho for Quahogs!
(Sing KO-hogs!)

I *could* run with gulls on the barrier sands,
Or skip wave-tossed stones that fit flat in my hands,
Or build dripsy castles, but I am *most* fond,
Of toeing for quahogs in Ninigret Pond.

I'll spy pointy oyster drills snailing their trails,
While goggle-eyed flounder scoot, rippling their tails,
In eelgrass beds, pipefish'll dart frond to frond—
When I toe for quahogs in Ninigret Pond.

Some folks gather steamers they dig by the peck,
That soft-shelled clam, deep in sand, stretching its neck,
But I'm glad to wade with no need for a spade,
My two feet in mud and my hat brim for shade,
'Round the bend to some sun-sparkled cove
and beyond—

I'm toeing for quahogs in Ninigret Pond!

—Leslie Bulion

The Last Passover

Greenwich, Connecticut

What happens when Elijah walks
Straight through the door
Off the Wilbur Cross Parkway?
No stealing sips of wine.
No lamb bones,
No bitter herbs or drowning parsley
In salt tears. No retelling
The old sad stories; no need
To eat unleavened bread.
No dancing on the far side of the Red Sea
While Egyptians are drowned.
Erase the Red x from the pre-fab front door;
Unask the four questions.
All the newborns are safe and
  the Angel
Of Death is just another winged
  Being,
As harmless as a moth.

—Liz Rosenberg

Holidays

The holiest of all holidays are those
  Kept by ourselves in silence and apart;
  The secret anniversaries of the heart,
  When the full river of feeling overflows;—
The happy days unclouded to their close;
  The sudden joys that out of darkness start
  As flames from ashes; swift desires that dart
  Like swallows singing down each wind that blows!

White as the gleam of a receding sail,
  White as a cloud that floats and fades in air,
  White as the whitest lily on a stream,
These tender memories are;—a Fairy Tale
  Of some enchanted land we know not where,
  But lovely as a landscape in a dream.

—Henry Wadsworth Longfellow

If I Had Nothing Else To Do, I'd Write a Christmas Card To **You**

If I had nothing else to do,

I'd write a Christmas card to you
But send it off to someone who,
Say, lived in Millinocket, Maine,
And very carefully explain
That she should quickly mail it on
By way of Portland, Oregon,
And when it got there they would know
To forward it to Buffalo,
New York, so that somebody there
Would have to send it first-class air
To Boston, Mass., and back again
By overnight delivery . . .
                              then
From Nashville, Tennessee, to Knox-
Ville, c/o of Auntie's P.O. box,
So she could zip it Fed Express
To your Chicago, Ill., address.
And someday, maybe mid-July—
A Christmas card! You'd wonder why
It took so long to get to you!
I'd call you up and tell you, too . . .,

If I had nothing else to do.

—*Mariel Bede*

The Menu at the First Thanksgiving, 1621

The Pilgrims likely brought no pigs across;
That first Thanksgiving they would eat no ham,
No mashed potato, sweet potato, yam,
For lack of sugar, no cranberry sauce.
Corn on the cob would not have been around.
A pumpkin pie? Not even in their dreams.
And yet the bounty was a match, it seems,
For this historic day on hallowed ground.
Wild turkey, goose, duck, swan, partridge and crane,
Cod, bass, herring, bluefish and eels released
Uncommon bonds of gratitude. That feast
Would be their last. They never met again—
The Indians and Pilgrims—to break bread.
But that Thanksgiving Day they were well-fed.

—*John Bucholz*

Boston

My northern pines are good enough for me,
But there's a town my memory uprears—
A town that always like a friend appears,
And always in the sunrise by the sea.
And over it, somehow, there seems to be
A downward flash of something new and fierce,
That ever strives to clear, but never clears
The dimness of a charmed antiquity.

—Edwin Arlington Robinson

At Boston Public Garden, Summer

Swans swim the pond
near paddle boats
shaped like swans.

Ducklings walk the lawn
next to sculptures
mimicking ducklings.

By Washington's statue
tourists make-believe
they're riding horses.

And children stretch
their shadows into
silver maple trees

whose own shadows
sway like children.

—Steven Withrow

Boston Marathon

feet feet feet feet feet feet feet feet
feet feet feet feet feet feet feet feet
coming   running   humbling   stumbling
down the down the down the down the
street   street   street   street   street
move push and strain not much remains
but still   the will   the beat beat beat
it's up ahead   the finish line   it's right
up there   keep going feet   keep going
feet feet feet feet feet   are crossing it
the FINISH line   the shine   the line!
feet!   feet!   feet!   FEAT!

—Kate Coombs

Boston Baked Beans: A Recipe

Soak two cups navy beans ovahnight in the Chahls Rivah.
Put beans in paht. Simmah 'til tendah.
On Satuhday mahnin' take T to Haymahket Skwayah.
Buy some bacon at the butchah theyah. Combine with beans in paht.
Locate the Stah Mahket neah Fenway Pahk. Fill caht with molasses,
dry mustahd, salt, peppah, onion, Wustasheah, ketchup, and brown sugah.
Combine with beans in paht. Bake until beans ah wicked tendah.
Three owahs. Maybe foah.

—David Elliott

Independence Day

To celebrate July the Fourth,
In Maine's "Downeast" (that's east coast, north),
Blueberry pancakes start the day
That ends with stars on Frenchman Bay.

Next, a street parade of floats,
Bagpipes, ponies, rolling boats,
Big kids-at-heart in go-kart cars,
All wend toward day's end under stars.

Lobster costumes, lobster treats,
Lobsters race in watery heats,
Race officials free the winner—
Lobster star won't end up dinner.

Cheers and smiles in salty air,
KA-BOOM! CRASH! SIZZLE! CRACKLE! FLARE!
A grand finale ends the day,
Exploding stars fill Frenchman Bay.

—*Leslie Bulion*

Watching the New Year's Eve Party Through the Staircase

Now midnight's here,
   The year is gone.
The merrymakers
   Carry on.

Instead of hats,
   They've sprouted horns
That make them look
   Like unicorns.

Tin whizzers buzz,
   Click-clackers clap,
Confetti snows
   Down Mrs. Knapp.

My Mother's fruitcakes
   Disappear.
The dancers shake
   The chandelier,

The floor, the windows . . .!
   Maybe this
Is why they stop
   Sometimes and kiss.

—*J. Patrick Lewis*

New England

Beach Days

Beaches are best on blue days:
sparkly crisp days
that tickle your skin with warmth.
"Wake up!" says the sun.
"Look at this! And this! And this!"
Blue beach days dazzle and tempt
with unspent gold.

But on gray days, beaches soothe.
"All the world is one," say the waves.
"Sky, sea, sand, it doesn't matter."
Gray beach days fill you up,
let you gaze and gaze
over the wide Atlantic
without shielding your eyes.

—Joyce Sidman

27

For Robert, Emily, and Walt

In Frost Country

When I see birches
dipping to earth from heaven
you're riding in them

And then you step down
from the crown   What care you take
that no branch will break

* *

Upstairs in Amherst

The whiteness of it
cries out   the curve of each sleeve
aches unceasingly

and every button
from neck to hemline   alive
burns in its prison

* *

Yawp

What road on this earth
is not blessed by the bootsoles
of your unbounded

song   or the hunger
of your time-traveling eyes
Walt   tender father

—Rhina P. Espaillat

28

The Continental Army

George Washington passes through
Lyme, CT, 10 April 1776

As I lifted the kettle from the hob,
I heard the sound of drums from far away.
I paused a moment. Then that hot water
got heavy. But I listened while I worked:
a steady rhythm, now and then a fife.
I washed, wiped and put the dishes away,
then dried my hands and hung up the dishrag.
Now I heard hoof beats and many men's boots.
I took my shawl and stepped into the dusk.

Out front, a white man with golden shoulders
and a sandy pigtail sat a gray horse
as if they were one being longing to prance.
Most of the town was lined along the street
clapping and cheering. A white army marched,
black booted feet in perfect unison,
toward the church, in identical cocked hats,
white sashes, blue coats with silver buttons,
fawn weskits and breeches, and knee high boots.
They carried muskets fitted with bayonets.
Never had I seen such terrible power.

They marched to the cadence the drummer set,
left right left right left right, for many ranks.
Some of us gathered behind McCurdy's house
whispering what we had heard and understood
of all this commotion. Zacheus swore
he saw some brothers among the soldiers.
The drummer they marched to brought up the rear.
We stood silenced when we saw his dark face.

—Marilyn Nelson

To Have and To Hold

On May 17th, two by two, side by side,
Surrounded by love, we were bursting with pride.
Eager for rights that were so long denied,
On May 17th, two by two, side by side,
Even newscasters grew misty-eyed
As each groom kissed his groom & each bride kissed her bride.
On May 17th, two by two, side by side,
Surrounded by love, we were bursting with pride.

—*Lesléa Newman*

Valentine

Chipmunks jump, and
Greensnakes slither
Rather burst than
Not be with her.

Bluebirds fight, but
Bears are stronger.
We've got fifty
Years or longer.

Hoptoads hop, but
Hogs are fatter.
Nothing else but
Us can matter.

—*Donald Hall*

Product

There is no beauty in New England like the boats.
Each itself, even the paint white
Dipping to each wave each time
At anchor, mast
And rigging tightly part of it
Fresh from the dry tools
And the dry New England hands.
The bow soars, finds the waves
The hull accepts. Once someone
Put a bowl afloat
And there for all to see, for all the children,
Even the New Englander
Was boatness. What I've seen
Is all I've found: myself.

—George Oppen

MID-ATL

The New Colossus

Not like the brazen giant of Greek fame,
With conquering limbs astride from land to land;
Here at our sea-washed, sunset gates shall stand
A mighty woman with a torch, whose flame
Is the imprisoned lightning, and her name
Mother of Exiles. From her beacon-hand
Glows world-wide welcome; her mild eyes command
The air-bridged harbor that twin cities frame.
"Keep, ancient lands, your storied pomp!" cries she
With silent lips. "Give me your tired, your poor,
Your huddled masses yearning to breathe free,
The wretched refuse of your teeming shore.
Send these, the homeless, tempest-tost to me,
I lift my lamp beside the golden door!"

—Emma Lazarus

Recuerdo

We were very tired, we were very merry—
We had gone back and forth all night on the ferry.
It was bare and bright, and smelled like a stable—
But we looked into a fire, we leaned across a table,
We lay on a hill-top underneath the moon;
And the whistles kept blowing, and the dawn came soon.

We were very tired, we were very merry—
We had gone back and forth all night on the ferry;
And you ate an apple, and I ate a pear,
From a dozen of each we had bought somewhere;
And the sky went wan, and the wind came cold,
And the sun rose dripping, a bucketful of gold.

We were very tired, we were very merry,
We had gone back and forth all night on the ferry.
We hailed, "Good morrow, mother!" to a shawl-covered head,
And bought a morning paper, which neither of us read;
And she wept, "God bless you!" for the apples and pears,
And we gave her all our money but our subway fares.

—*Edna St. Vincent Millay*

September Twelfth, 2001

Two caught on film who hurtle
   from the eighty-second floor,
choosing between a fireball
and to jump holding hands,

aren't us. I wake beside you,
stretch, scratch, taste the air,
   the incredible joy of coffee
and the morning light.

Alive, we open eyelids
on our pitiful share of time,
we bubbles rising and bursting
   in a boiling pot.

—*X. J. Kennedy*

Ellis Island
Mathematics

The old world scrambles
for purchase in the new,
holding on with broken fingernails.

The cuticles of travel raw,
bloody, chewed down, but still
we are safer here, or so we believe.

Here in the squawling ranks
of immigrants, the family is cattle
fearing the knacker's knife.

More feared, though, are the knives
of the horsemen of the steppes,
the unknown safer than the known.

The family tries on new names
as easily as a lady of means
tries a hat at the milliner's.

Lev becomes Louis, Lou.
Richil Rose, Aron Harry.
My father, Wolf, tamed into Will.

Is it Yolin, Jolin, Yole? Manifest
transliterations change vowels,
consonants, till we all sound American.

Till we are all sound Americans,
only Jewish by extraction, attraction,
subtraction—Ellis Island Mathematics.

—*Jane Yolen*

An Irish Emigrant
Bound for America

It's not the siren song of common prayer
That summons up the confidence to go.
He hears the ancient voice of some forebear,

A victim of repression and despair,
Who tells him everything he needs to know.
It's not the siren song of common prayer.

From Dublin to the coast of County Clare,
America that calls by radio
Is but the ancient voice of some forebear

Repeating "Oppurtunity goes there!
Git on with it, me lad, you'll miss the show."
It's not the siren song of common prayer.

"Hearts are sad, potato cellars bare,
The future's quick as coffins down below."
He hears the ancient voice of his forebear.

"Us Irish niver knew a millionaire.
   Git goin', even if you have to row"
Is not the siren song of common prayer.
He hears the ancient voice of his forebear.

—*Mariel Bede*

Bringing Palestine Home to America

At Kennedy Airport my heart was the biggest suitcase I brought.
In it I put whole cities folded tightly like pants and shirts.
I brought all of my people with me.
The first amendment granted me the right of peaceable assembly
So I began to assemble my refugee-immigrant world—
With many pieces missing I found close replacements.
I gave myself a globe and with a bold font added Palestine to it.
I put Band-Aids on the world's torn cities.
I labeled the door to my apartment: Jaffa Gate,
Called my tiny kitchen Old Jerusalem.
My bedroom's name became Ramallah,
The balcony Jabal Al Carmel
And the River Jordan the water faucet.
Every morning I placed my finger on the globe
where the Middle East is and announced: *Good morning all of M.E.,*
I want to let you know that American me is fine.
I heard no response but for the duration of that imagination
I won over my sense of alienation and belonged peaceably and freely
with everything and everyone in silence—
the language with no dialects, accents, places of origin,
or destinations.

— *Ibtisam Barakat*

إحضار فلسطين إلى منزلي في أمريكا

النص الأصلي للقصيدة بالإنجليزية، والترجمة للعربية، كلاهما
للشاعرة الفلسطينية الأمريكية ابتسام بركات

حين وَصَلتُ إلى مطار كنيدي في نيويورك
كان قلبي أكبر حقيبة سَفَر أحضرتُها معي.
فيه طويتُ مُدناً كاملة
مثلما طَويتُ السّراويلَ والقمصان.
لقد أحضرتُ معي كل الفلسطينيين. . .
وبما أن الدستور الأمريكي يمنح
حق التجمع السّلمي للمواطنين،
صرتُ أجمّع حُطام عالمي . . .
وجَدتُ البدائل للقطع المفقودة الكثيرة.
أشتريتُ مُجسّم الكرة الأرضية،
وبِخَط عريض أضفتُ فلسطين. . .
وعلى جراح المدن الممزقة
وضعتُ لاصقات إسعاف طبية.
أطلقتُ على مَدخل منزلي: باب العامود.
وصارَ اسمُ مطبخي الصغير: القدس العتيقة.
غرفة النوم الصَقتُ عليها يافطة: مدينة رام الله.
جبل الكرمل صار اسم البلكونة العالية.
ونهر الأردن صنبور المياه.
كل صباح وضعتُ اصبعي على الكرة الأرضية
حيثُ "الشرق الأوسط" وهتفت:
عمْتَ صباحاً يا عالمي وأيتها الانسانية!
أخبرُكَم أني الآن في الولايات المتحدة الأمريكية.
وحين لم أسمع الاّ السّكون يملأ الكون طمأنينة،
انتصرْتُ للحظة على الغربَة اللغوية
وعرفتُ معنى أن أنتمي بحرّية
مع كل الأشياء وكل الكائنات
في لغة الصّمت التي تصغي بلا حدود
ولا تعرف اللّهجات
ولا اللّكنات
ولا الأصول العرقية
ولا وجهات السفر
ولا المطارات الدولية . . .

—*Translation by Ibtisam Barakat*

BILLIE HOLIDAY
1915–1959

Lady **Day**

On "Blue Moon" nights I love to hypnotize
Strangers in smoky nightclubs just like this.
"Too Marvelous for Words" in "Them There Eyes,"
They swoon like I was "Prelude to a Kiss."
"Nice Work If You Can Get It." What I've got,
Oh no, "You Can't Take That Away From Me."
It's "All Or Nothing At All"—or maybe not—
"I Gotta Right to Sing the Blues" off-key.
"What Is This Thing Called Love?" I cannot find
It in a blessed note a Lady sings.
A life mistreated treats you so unkind,
Left me with "Just One of Those (Crazy) Things"—
A voice that Harlem toned to living tuned,
A voice I carry with me like a wound.

—*Peggy Gifford*

Eliza, Age 10, Harlem

I'm not like they say,
those withered onions on the stoop
clucking their sorrowful tongues.
I'm concentrated. I'm a sweet
package of love. Jesus

says so, and He's better than the angels
'cause He knows how to die;
He suffers the children
to come to Him.
I can climb these stairs—

easy, even in T-straps. Yes,
I am my grandma's sugar pea
and someday I'm gonna pop
right out—and then, boys,
you better jump back!

—*Rita Dove*

Poets House

Where do poems go when they roam?
To Poets House where they are home!
With 60,000 books to read—
Satisfying every need.
Workshops, readings, poems on tape.
Come to learn or just escape.
Join talks, and panels, seminars too.
Lovely book art is on view.
A clearinghouse for information.
For kids there's Inspiration Station
Where children's books sit on low shelves
And kids can write poems by themselves.
A home for poems that's so aesthetic—
So come on down and get poetic!

—Douglas Florian

POETS HOUSE IS A NATIONAL POETRY LIBRARY
AND LITERARY CENTER IN NEW YORK CITY.

Triolet

Should men govern without consent?
  Suffrage is the pivotal right
We must express our discontent
When men govern without consent
Let's gather at the voting tent
Amendments are what we must write
When men govern without consent
  Suffrage is the pivotal right

—Tricia Stohr-Hunt

SUSAN B. ANTHONY
1820–1906

New York Notes

1.
Caught on a side street
in heavy traffic, I said
to the cabbie, I should
have walked. He replied,
I should have been a doctor.

2.
When can I get on the 11:33
I ask the guy in the information booth
at the Atlantic Avenue Station.
When the doors open, he says.
I am home among my people.

—Harvey Shapiro

Fish Tales

Chinatown haul—
   soft-shell crabs and lobsters:
    non-refundable.

New Chinese takeout
   three glads withering near
    the cash register.

—Sydell Rosenberg

High-Rise
Window Washer

I'm a window wiper
A squeegee swiper
A scraper in the sky.
Just one good squirt
Gets rid of dirt
Six hundred six feet high.

Up with the birds
Few words are heard
So high above the ground.
And let me school
You to one rule:
Be sure you don't look down!

—Douglas Florian

New Year's Eve:
A 21st Century Ball Drop

The air is cold.
The crowd is thick.
But it doesn't matter,
when on December 31st
Times Square becomes a theatre:
For 100 years and more
people have not stopped
welcoming the New Year there
just as a ball is dropped!

Now in its second century,
the ball is 12 feet wide:
a ball of crystal triangles!
L-E-D lights sparkle inside.
The crowd counts down the last seconds,
as the Old Year becomes past tense.
A computer lowers the ball:
    glittering...
      gorgeous...
        immense!

—*Bobbi Katz*

Asian Market

The tired edges of any town, many towns.
Strip mall after strip mall, all so alike
that they become invisible.

The sign says *Asian Market*.
It ought to say *Emporium!*
with slash and stop for emphasis,
because of what's inside:

Smells. Soy and garlic, ginger and seaweed,
cabbage singing backup a little too loud.

Kimchi in jars, sizes fistful to bucket.
Bags of rice plump as a healthy child.
Noodles. Noodles. Noodles. Noodles.
Bamboo: bowls and mats and spoons.

Sweets in a pink and green box
with a secret: *You can eat the wrapper.*

The cellophane crackles,
then disappears on your tongue.
A small moment of magic
in the back seat of the car.

—*Linda Sue Park*

동양 마켓
-뉴욕주 로체스터 교외에서-　　　　　린다 수 박

피로해 보이는 도시 변두리
많은 도시 변두리
길가에 줄 지어선 상점들
계속 늘어선 상점들
다들 비슷해서 눈에 안 띈다

간판은 동양 마켓
진열된 상품만 보아도
사선과 마침표로 강조한 자파점!

냄새들, 간장과 마늘, 생강과 미역
배추가 부르는 백업 노래소리는 좀 노프다

김치병들은 주먹만한것으로 부터 양동이 만한것까지
건강한 아이들 같이 통통한 쌀 자루들
국수, 냉면, 당면, 소면
대나무: 그릇들과 깔개 또 수까락들

분홍과 초록의 작은 상자속에든 사탕의 비밀:
먹어도 되는 겁대기
그 투명 종이는 바스락 하면서
혀 위에서 사라진다.

차 뒷자리에서 맛보는
이 신기한 순간!

—*Translation by Linda Sue Park*

Never Say No

It's messy, delicious . . . a perfect bite
Never say no to a Philly cheesesteak
Chipped beef and onions, grilled just right
It's messy, delicious, a perfect bite
It will have you believing in love at first sight!
The chewy roll and gooey cheese make
it messy, delicious—a perfect bite
Never say no to a Philly cheesesteak!

—*Laura Purdie Salas*

Ode to a Knish Shop

Mrs. Stahl's sold kasha knishes,
Boy oh boy, were they delicious!
When I was young, they cost a nickel
(cheaper than a kosher pickle).
In Brighton Beach, beneath the el,
seduced by that arresting smell,
I'd take the last place in the queue
on Coney Island Avenue
then perch upon a worn red stool
and try my hardest not to drool
as I watched Mrs. Stahl herself
pluck knishes from a metal shelf.
She served them piping hot with pride
(the sign outside bragged "Baked Not Fried").
The pastry, bigger than my fist
caressed my tongue, like being kissed.
The outside dough was parchment-thin
yet strong enough to hold within
buckwheat groats that smelled of earth
and added inches to my girth.
But in those days I didn't care
a whit about my derriére.
That kasha knish was heaven-sent,
no nickel ever better spent.

—Lesléa Newman

The Great **Hudson River Revival**

The Clearwater Festival takes place at the historic river park Croton Point in Croton-on-Hudson, New York. It became one of the most important music festivals in the United States. Pete Seeger and the Clearwater were the engines for the Clean Water Act.

A banjo player named Pete Seeger
Loved the Hudson, thought it's sad
To see it dying from pollution.
What a good idea he had:
Build a boat to save a river!
A handsome sloop like those once used
For moving freight along the Hudson
Years before it was abused.
Build a boat to save a river!
Bring attention to the glory
Of a river where life prospered,
Of a river with a story!
That's how the sloop Clearwater
Was built & came to be
The force behind the revival
That everyone can see.
Each June for almost 50 years
There's a week long celebration
Of the Hudson—once polluted—
Now a model for the nation!

—Bobbi Katz

Niagara Falls

When we left the Old World,
we hoped to find our own vision of paradise—
the bedrock of something new and vast—
but explorers, daydreamers, seekers
of the Fountain of Youth
could never have imagined *this*—
a cascading chasm churning off the edge of
our old maps,
a three-fall wall of water
large enough for Lady Liberty herself
to bathe in,

tumbling in the steady hoof beat rhythm
of bison and mustangs yet to be found,
rumbling with
the hungry purr of trains racing west,
the metallic reverberation of factories, cars,
even the deep, mournful calls of Jazz—
a fountain bigger than we could dream,
inspiration wild
and fast
and plentiful enough
for a story as new as the land.

—P. Maxwell Towler

Spellbound

Scripps National Spelling Bee
Oxon Hill, Maryland

Shaking, yet filled with anticipation, we're
Performing on TV before the nation!
Entrants have
Learned
Long words
Intelligently, and
Now it is my turn to spell out
Grandiloquently.
But should it be I or does
E follow D? One of those letters will
Eliminate me . . .

—Avis Harley

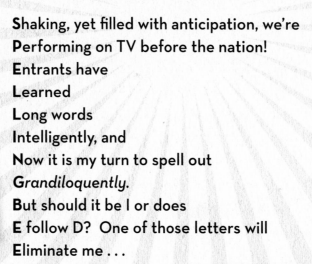

213
LENA

Groundhognostication

Punxsutawney, Pennsylvania
February 2

Gobbler's Knob lies blanketed in February snow,
but even in the biting cold, people's faces glow.

They've travelled here from far and wide to celebrate together,
and listen as the groundhog gives his verdict on the weather.

They join in the festivities as bands play on for hours,
while Punxsutawney Phil warms up his shadow-reading powers.

Finally, the main event – the "groundhognostication!"
Mittened fingers cross in hopes of spring's initiation.

Will they suffer six more weeks of winter's frigid gloom?
Maybe yes, or maybe no, but soon bright buds will bloom.

—B. J. Lee

Champion Betty

The Westminster Kennel Club Dog Show

My name is "Dame Elizabeth
McWaggleton Confetti
Lucinda Rainbow Barksalot"
(but you can call me Betty).

My lineage is excellent,
a purebred pedigree.
Great-grandma was the Best in Show
in Nineteen Eighty-Three.

I primly prance around the ring,
then strike a stately pose.
A judge inspects my canine form
and rates me, tail to nose.

And if I win I'll be the toast
of all of New York City.
And every TV talk-show host
will tell me that I'm pretty.

But even if I fail to win
I'll wag my tail with pride.
I'm more than just a show dog. I'm
a champion inside.

—Allan Wolf

Silent Sentinel

Battle of Gettysburg

At field's edge atop Cemetery Ridge, an old,
battered tree stands—split down the middle like
so many families whose sons
went separate ways in war.

Silent sentinel, it saw that costliest of campaigns—
an eternity of suffering in three days' time.
Unmovable witness, it watched Pickett's charge,
counted up its colossal casualties.

With roots bathed in bloodshed—
did it break at once or over time, riven by
the weight of sorrow, torn apart by conflicting
passions of thousands injured and dead?

Still it stands, an aged, living monument
in a park full of granite and bronze markers.
One by one, in time, witness trees fall,
the last living veterans who survived it all.

—Kelly Fineman

Kishacoquillas
Valley Ride

When we visit the valley, my Amish cousin hitches up
the mare. Climb in, he says. I take a giant step

into the black buggy—then turn to lift
my sisters up. My cousin lets me sit in front.

We start with a jerk, then swerve onto the road.
Once we've straightened out, he lets me hold

the reins. Feeling grownup and almost Amish,
I'm suddenly shy. It's hard to hear each other

speak—the steel wheels make such a racket
on the road. Looking past the horse's rump

I watch the road crawl under us, the fields
part on either side, slow my breath, and wonder

how it would feel to live like this, content,
beside my Amish cousin at this pace.

—Ann Hostetler

Beach Day

Island Beach State Park, New Jersey

We leave home before dawn, our car packed
with towels, sunblock, coolers of food.

There are closer beaches,
but they're for boardwalk people.

We smile when we reach the park gate.
No hotels here. No tourist shops.

Can you smell the salt air? Mom asks.
The beach stays hidden behind miles of dunes.

At last, Dad finds a spot. We tumble out of the car,
race down a path through the scrub.

There! I am first to glimpse the wide, white beach,
first to stick my toes in the icy Atlantic.

I stretch my arms and spin. All I see are the dunes
and the ocean. All I hear is the music of the waves.

—Laura Shovan

Water, Water Everywhere:
A Delaware Chant

Delaware River,
Garrisons Lake,
Broad Creek slithers
like a snake

Nanticoke River,
Chesapeake Bay,
Atlantic Ocean,
cold and grey

Breakers and currents
kidnap sand,
Neptune's stealing
Delaware's land

—Laura Purdie Salas

Right Time, Right Place

Red Knots don't have a map
to guide them to Delaware Bay.
What leads them, hungry and thin,
so far up the coast each May?

Horseshoe crabs don't plan to prepare
a feast for the birds when they land.
What pulls them from the sea
to bury millions of eggs in the sand?

A full moon shines on Delaware Bay.
Two species meet. Then one
heads back to sea and the other,
grown fat and strong, flies on.

—Helen Frost

Mural Compass

Tall figures rise from city ground.
They speak to me without a sound
from vibrant faces, facing sun—
these paintings are for everyone.

Chartreuse and purple pop the street,
kaleidoscoping at my feet.
Graffiti marks are now long gone.
These paintings are for everyone.

On buildings bare and bridges wide
where history and hope collide
shine songs of freedom, fame, and fun—
These paintings are for everyone.

—Robyn Hood Black

THE WORLD'S LARGEST OUTDOOR ART PROJECT, PHILADELPHIA, PENNSYLVANIA

City of **Brotherly Love**

Buzzing around Doug's birthday party with the alacrity
of an over caffeinated bee, clutching fistfuls of tickets
to play more free video games, I dart to the bathroom
to empty my soda-filled belly when two older kids,
stringy haired and dotted with acne, bump into me,
stare into my eyes, chuckle, then unleash a word
I had never felt the venom of prior to that moment.
It has six letters, two syllables, and one punch to my soul.
I freeze in shock as they walk out the door, my mocha-
colored skin burns red with anger, my face turned
downward in shame.

—Charles Waters

Black Boys Play the Classics

The most popular "act" in
Penn Station
is the three black kids in ratty
sneakers & T-shirts playing
two violins and a cello—Brahms.
White men in business suits
have already dug into their pockets
as they pass and they toss in
a dollar or two without stopping.
Brown men in work-soiled khakis
stand with their mouths open,
arms crossed on their bellies
as if they themselves have always
wanted to attempt those bars.
One white boy, three, sits
cross-legged in front of his
idols—in ecstasy—
their slick, dark faces,
their thin, wiry arms,
who must begin to look
like angels!
Why does this trembling
pull us?
A: *Beneath the surface we are one.*
B: *Amazing! I did not think that
they could speak this tongue.*

—*Toi Derricotte*

The Strand Theater

Wildwood by-the-Sea, New Jersey

Saturday sun steams
from the wooden planks
and concrete of the boardwalk,
we slip into the cool cavern
of the Strand, rumba
down the aisle in the buttered
darkness to the sound of
Raisinets, Dots, and Goobers
rattling in their boxes,
fold down the creaky plush seats,
sit in air-conditioned
expectation, watch for the heavy
velvet curtains to sweep
aside . . . .

—*Joan Bransfield Graham*

53

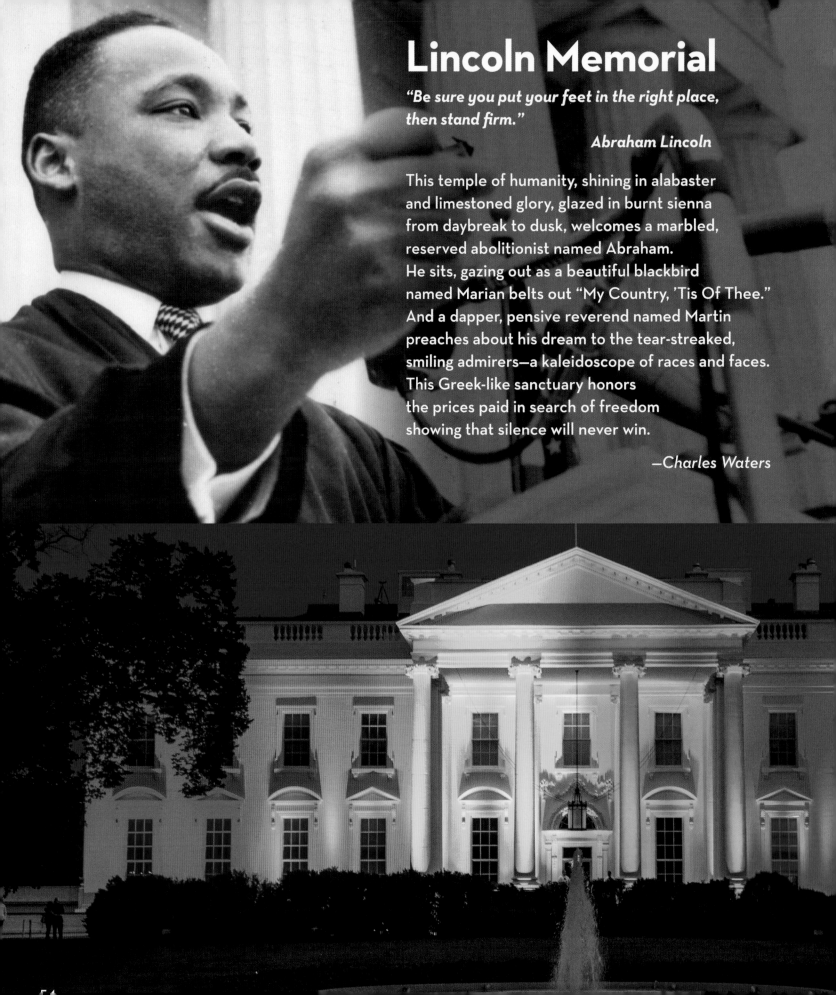

Lincoln Memorial

"Be sure you put your feet in the right place,
then stand firm."

Abraham Lincoln

This temple of humanity, shining in alabaster
and limestoned glory, glazed in burnt sienna
from daybreak to dusk, welcomes a marbled,
reserved abolitionist named Abraham.
He sits, gazing out as a beautiful blackbird
named Marian belts out "My Country, 'Tis Of Thee."
And a dapper, pensive reverend named Martin
preaches about his dream to the tear-streaked,
smiling admirers—a kaleidoscope of races and faces.
This Greek-like sanctuary honors
the prices paid in search of freedom
showing that silence will never win.

—Charles Waters

That April Train

The train carrying Abraham Lincoln's coffin from Washington, D.C.

That April train coming slow
around the curve of history.
We hear it rattling the tracks,
lonesome dirge on the rails.

The old man's picture
fastened to the front,
like an angel above
the cattle car as warning.

His long face, made longer
by the draw of war.
He knew that bullet
was his and did not flinch.

The last man to die
in the battle of brothers,
excepting the black men
hanging from the trees,

Except our hearts darkened,
except our history stretched
on the rack of hate.
Accept all that.

—Jane Yolen

The White House

Its white exterior reflects a rainbow of colors,
sometimes literally as it is lit in celebration
of events. Permanent in a way that its occupants
cannot be, the White House is also a metaphor
for the office of its resident, the President who
represents all citizens, regardless of religion or
race, politics or persuasion, age or ancestry.

"Whisper White," its walls contain generations
of first-family secrets, from Abigail Adams's un-
mentionables drying in the East Room to the
incapacities experienced by Presidents. Strong
enough to bear the weight of crippling sorrows, from
the loss of Lincoln to the tragedies of terrorist
attacks and wars. Grand enough for a king, yet
not a palace; our head of state is simply a citizen,
who will return to a simpler house in due time.

—Kelly Fineman

The Underground Railroad

This way. That star, your ticket.
Find the shadows. Take the creek.
That barn, a station. This way, you be the fog.
Sleep by day, slip out by night,
Stay low and skirt the fields.
Behind that house, across the washing porch,
an entrance.
In the basket, bread. Warm stew.
Avoid the main roads, catchers cagey.
Slide through silence, ease the squeaky gates.
Down that lane, a bendy tree.
A wrought iron fence. Look for a rag.
Inside, a cellar you can trust.
Nightfall, head out through the high corn, find
    the shed.
Pull the tarp up, there you wait.
Be getting cold now, take this wrap.
Look for a steeple, go 'round back.
Tap twice and you'll find mercy.
Over yonder. A stall. A coop. A cave.
Get you to the river. Give a whistle.
You gon' make it. *Shhh*.
This way.

—*Sara Holbrook*

Note to Nature Regarding **Cherry Blossoms**

To make this air beautiful,
fill it with blossom bouquets;
name them cherry and dot them on branches.
Invite them to welcome spring
with tender shades of blush and pink;
Send invitations to sightseers and travelers.
Tell them to hurry.

—*Rebecca Kai Dotlich*

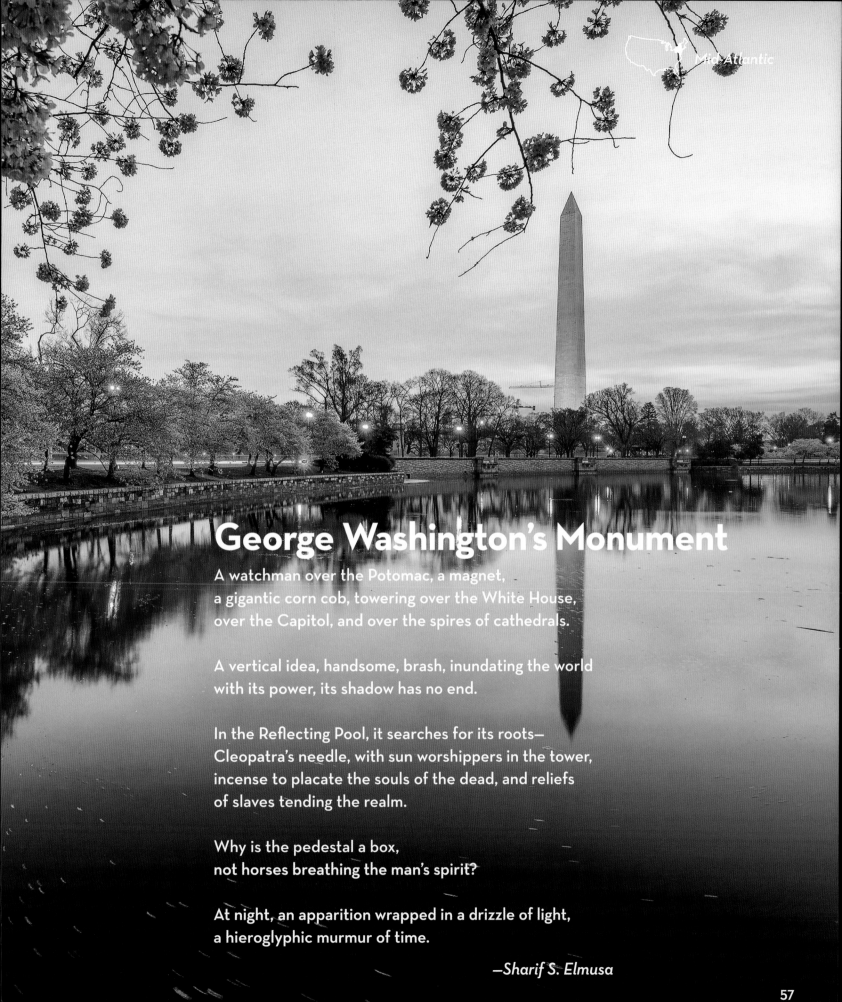

George Washington's Monument

A watchman over the Potomac, a magnet,
a gigantic corn cob, towering over the White House,
over the Capitol, and over the spires of cathedrals.

A vertical idea, handsome, brash, inundating the world
with its power, its shadow has no end.

In the Reflecting Pool, it searches for its roots—
Cleopatra's needle, with sun worshippers in the tower,
incense to placate the souls of the dead, and reliefs
of slaves tending the realm.

Why is the pedestal a box,
not horses breathing the man's spirit?

At night, an apparition wrapped in a drizzle of light,
a hieroglyphic murmur of time.

—*Sharif S. Elmusa*

SOUTH

EAST

One Minute Till **Sunrise**

The morning river wears its blanket of fog,
the town its necklace of lights,
the sky its sweater of cloud,
the grass its slicker of dew,
the trees a mist of new leaves,
and the birds their sweet halos of song.

It is spring—one minute till sunrise.
Whispers of breeze,
secrets in shadows.
Who dares tell the great sun
how perfect it all already is?

—Marc Harshman

Blue Ridge Mountains

The native Powhatan
named these blue-washed mountains *Quirank*.
A road snakes round a valley of trees
blue as ocean from a breath of branches.
Pines breathe in
and out a blue fog.
A story behind each name—
Humpback Rock, Bearwallow Gap:
stones breaching waves of morning haze;
black bears wallowing in cold springs
rolling and rooting in the ooze.
Slabs of bedrock appearing
and reappearing like magic
pumiced by showers and gusting wind

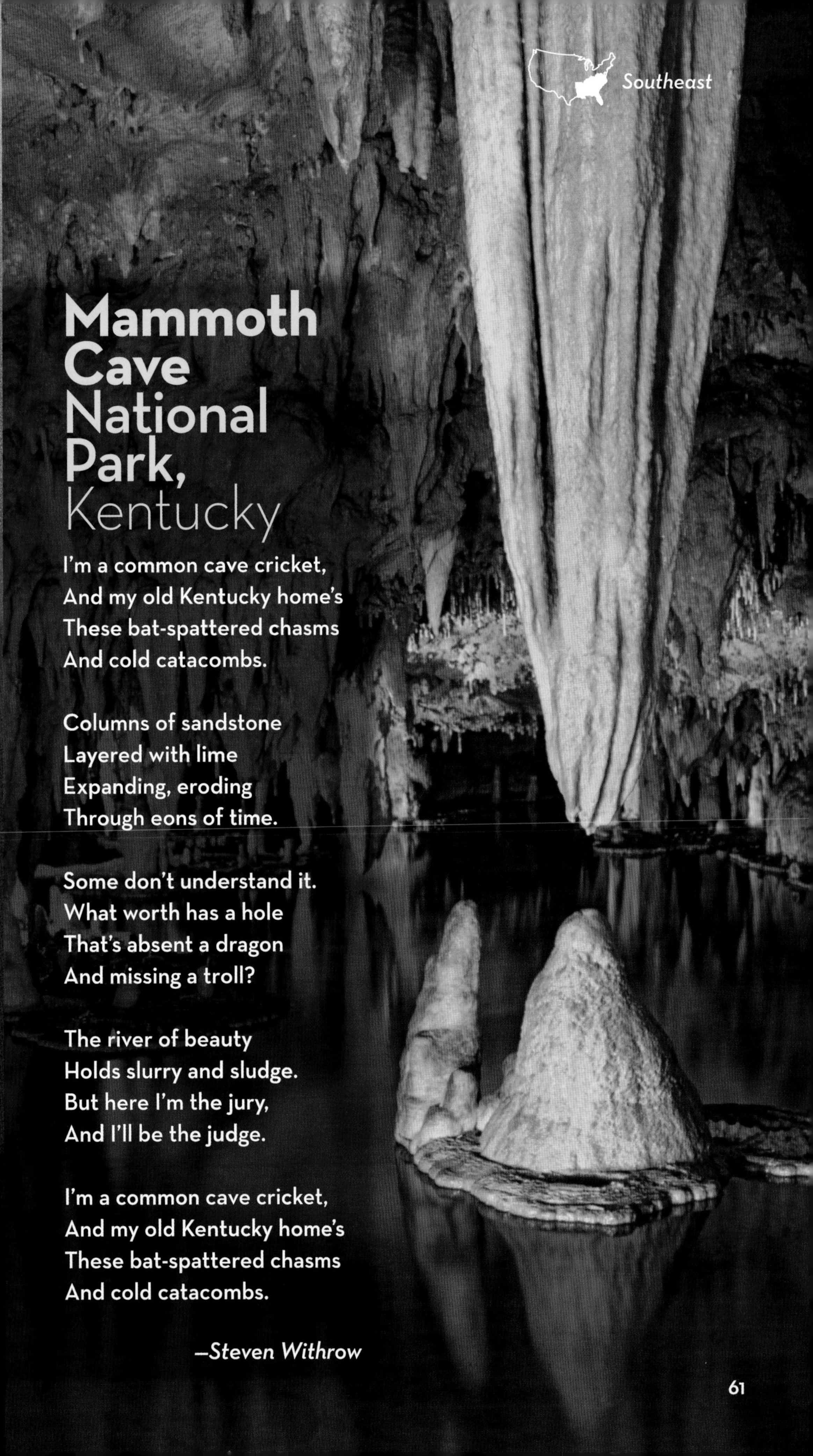

Mammoth Cave National Park, Kentucky

I'm a common cave cricket,
And my old Kentucky home's
These bat-spattered chasms
And cold catacombs.

Columns of sandstone
Layered with lime
Expanding, eroding
Through eons of time.

Some don't understand it.
What worth has a hole
That's absent a dragon
And missing a troll?

The river of beauty
Holds slurry and sludge.
But here I'm the jury,
And I'll be the judge.

I'm a common cave cricket,
And my old Kentucky home's
These bat-spattered chasms
And cold catacombs.

—Steven Withrow

ELVIS PRESLEY
1935-1977

Standing Outside
Graceland

The castle of the King
of Rock 'n' Roll–
Mama says the name
she whispers like a prayer–
Graceland.
There, just beyond this fieldstone wall.

Records gold, carpets white.
Rhinestone bathed in neon light.
Well, that's all right, Mama.
That's all right.

Mama says the King was born
a dirt-poor boy
like me
before he called this castle home
here in Memphis, Tennessee.

A thousand dreams to fill the night.
A mama's arms to hold him tight.
Well, that's all right, Mama.
That's all right.

—*Eric Ode*

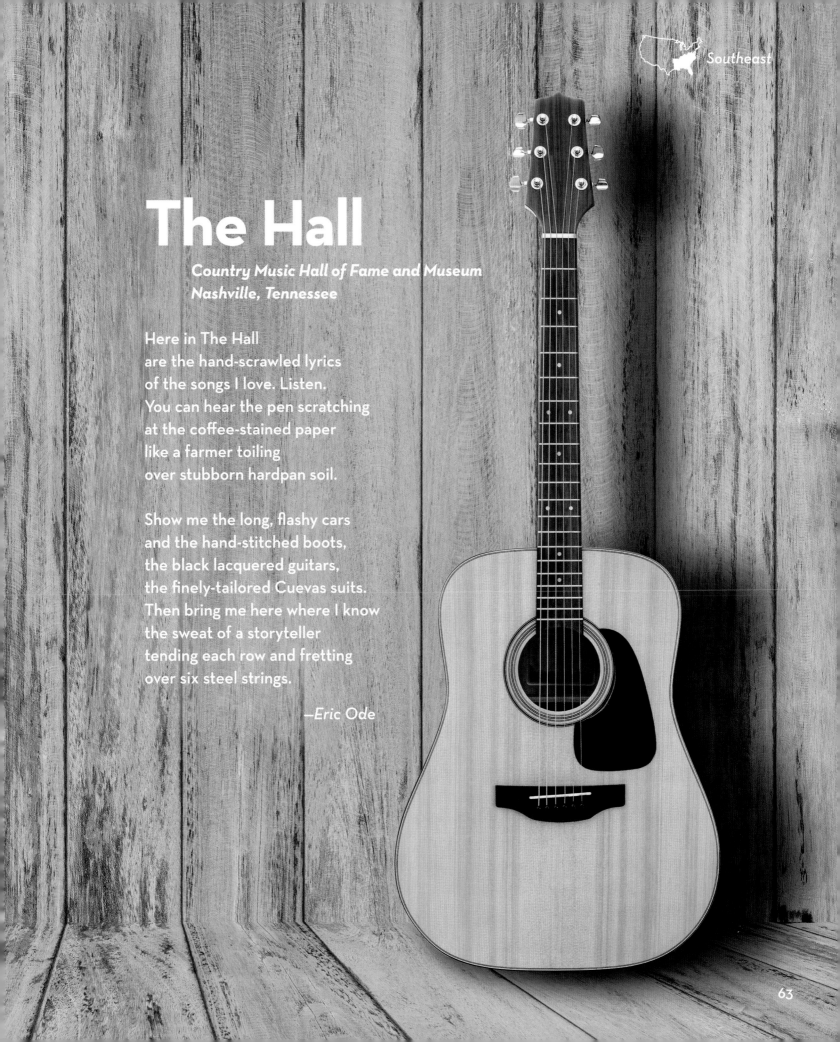

The Hall

Country Music Hall of Fame and Museum
Nashville, Tennessee

Here in The Hall
are the hand-scrawled lyrics
of the songs I love. Listen.
You can hear the pen scratching
at the coffee-stained paper
like a farmer toiling
over stubborn hardpan soil.

Show me the long, flashy cars
and the hand-stitched boots,
the black lacquered guitars,
the finely-tailored Cuevas suits.
Then bring me here where I know
the sweat of a storyteller
tending each row and fretting
over six steel strings.

—Eric Ode

Birmingham

The farm has charm,
But I like gritty.
I like the sounds
Of the soulful city.

I like the mountains.
I like the sea,
But the beat of the street
Is music to me.

I like to travel.
I like to roam,
But the sound of the city
Calls me home.

—*Charles Ghigna*

City
Home

My city is bursting with treasures.
Pigeons peck crumbs in the rain.
The man on my corner sells flowers.
I travel to school on a train.

Musicians sing songs on the sidewalk.
Small children play ball in the park.
Listen. You'll hear every language.
It never gets lonely or dark.

I like when I visit the country.
It's neat to look up at the stars.
But I always miss these tall buildings.
And I miss the sound of the cars.

—*Amy Ludwig VanDerwater*

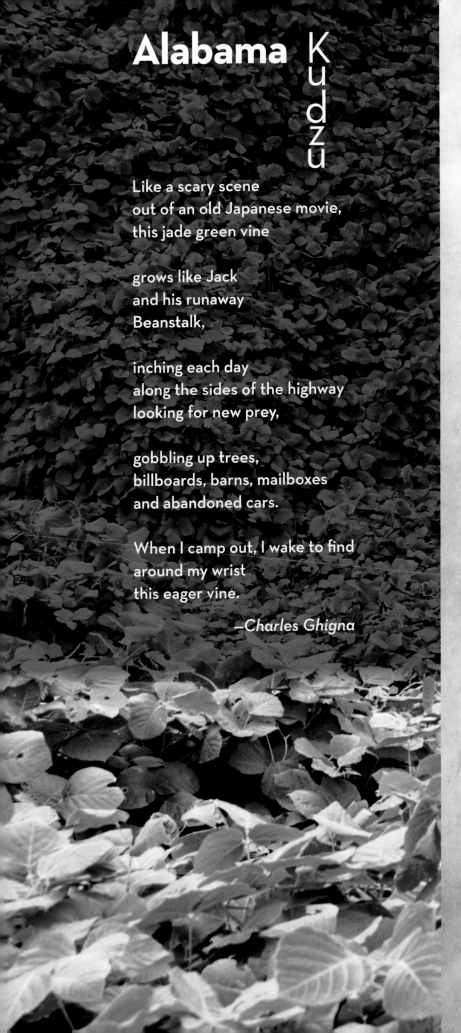

Alabama Kudzu

Like a scary scene
out of an old Japanese movie,
this jade green vine

grows like Jack
and his runaway
Beanstalk,

inching each day
along the sides of the highway
looking for new prey,

gobbling up trees,
billboards, barns, mailboxes
and abandoned cars.

When I camp out, I wake to find
around my wrist
this eager vine.

—Charles Ghigna

Daybreak in Alabama

When I get to be a composer
I'm gonna write me some music about
Daybreak in Alabama
And I'm gonna put the purtiest songs in it
Rising out of the ground like a swamp mist
And falling out of heaven like soft dew.
I'm gonna put some tall tall trees in it
And the scent of pine needles
And the smell of red clay after rain
And long red necks
And poppy colored faces
And big brown arms
And the field daisy eyes
Of black and white black white black people
And I'm gonna put white hands
And black hands and brown and yellow hands
And red clay earth hands in it
Touching everybody with kind fingers
And touching each other natural as dew
In that dawn of music when I
Get to be a composer
And write about daybreak
In Alabama.

—Langston Hughes

The Derby

All the members of the band have finally memorized
"My Old Kentucky Home."

TV cameras zero in on nervous owners wearing
lucky socks and ties.

In the jocks' room, riders slide into their splendid,
ridiculous silks.

On the backstretch a groom in an ancient baseball cap
whispers to a chestnut colt: "Remember what we talked

about? Lot of pretty ladies in big hats out there today.
You keep your mind on business."

—Ron Koertge

If The **Court** **Could Speak**

If the court could speak
what would it say?

Would it speak of the skill,
the will on display?

Would it rattle off names
that put on a show?

Like Main Event,
Booger, Predator, Alimoe?

Would it recount battles
won and lost?

Would it speak of respect
earned and hard fought?

Would it tell tall tales
of aerial artistry?

Would it share stories of friends
who were once enemies?

Would it speak of the love
exhibited each play?

If the court could speak
what would it say?

—*Charles R. Smith Jr.*

Nicknames in the NBA

(A Found Poem)

The Mailman, The Admiral,
The Answer, The Truth,
The Waiter, The Mayor,
The Dream, The Sheriff,
The Goods, The Glove.
Big Ticket, Big Country,
Big Smooth, Big Nasty.
Zo, Bo, Mo, Lo, Stro,
Rip, Tip, Pip.
Cat, Dog, Snake, Pig, Bull, Horse.
Sam I Am, Tim Bug, Tin Man,
Thunder Dan, Vinsanity,
Mt. Motumbo, White Chocolate,
Human Highlight Film.
Tractor, Scooter,
Ukraine Train, Hot Rod.
Shaq, KD. The Splash Brothers.
Wow! Yao!
The Chosen One.
His Airness.

—*Anonymous*

It Must Be **Halloween**

Jack-o-lanterns grin with light.
Shrieks and laughter fill the night.
We're ruining our appetite.
It must be Halloween.

A wrinkled ghost skips up the walk.
A doorbell rings. A knuckle knocks.
A zombie answers! What a shock!
It must be Halloween.

Nuns and ninjas walk the street.
A werewolf howls out, "Trick-or-treat!"
A tiny Batman falls asleep.
It must be Halloween.

We head home after one last door.
Our bags are full. Our feet are sore.
We spread our treasure on the floor,
a week of stomach aches in store!

It must be Halloween.

—Allan Wolf

Ozark Hills

Motorcycles zoom down pig trails and twisting roads.
Beware, wildlife will knock at the door or hide inside.
Arkansas dumb laws: don't wake up a bear to photograph,
or an alligator in your bathtub. Diamond digging
is allowed in a mud field, as is catching fish in the rain.
Wild persimmon fruit predicts winter, seed-shaped
spoon, deep snow, or a fork, mild winter. Flatlanders
and hill people eat, poke sallet, muscadine, pawpaws,
wild hog, squirrel with dumplings, and drink, sweet tea.
Ghosts roam buildings while Boggy Creek Monster
wanders aimlessly. Old witches do hocus pocus,
and turkeys fly during Turkey Trot Festival.

—Mary Nida Smith

The Biltmore House

This massive house, in chateau style,
was home to husband, wife, and child.
The babe was born to coos and cheers,
and took her very first steps here.
They hung their portraits on these walls.
They talked and walked along these halls.
They laughed and raced the marble stair.
Lean in close, you'll hear them there.
This house of wonder, spires, and domes:
One family simply called it "home."

—*Allan Wolf*

THE LARGEST PRIVATELY OWNED HOUSE IN AMERICA
ASHEVILLE, NORTH CAROLINA

HELEN KELLER
1880-1968

Listening

My fingers listen
to a wave of vibrations:
an ocean of sounds—
    convergence of rhythms
    violas, cornets, and drums
Each impassioned note
satisfies silence in the soul:
glorious surprise—
    my heart thrums—the melody
    flowing from the radio

—Linda Kulp Trout

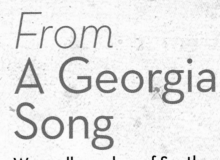

Swamp Song

The swamp speaks Geechee Gulla
And the frogs stamp their flat feet.
No one owns the land.
No one owns the land.
So hum the dragonflies,
Dancing above
Like flying jewels,
Like the fingers of sweet grass weavers
Restlessly at rest.

—Liz Rosenberg

From A Georgia Song

We swallow odors of Southern cities,
Fatback boiled to submission,
Tender evening poignancies of
Magnolia and the great green
Smell of fresh sweat.
In Southern fields,
The sound of distant
Feet running or dancing,
And the liquid notes of
Sorrow songs,
Waltzes, screams and
French quadrilles float over
The loam of Georgia.

Sing me to sleep Savannah.
. . .
Cry for our souls, Augusta.
. . .
Dare us new dreams, Columbus.
. . .
O Atlanta, O deep, and
Once lost city,

Chant for us a new song. A song
Of Southern peace.

—Maya Angelou

No Mistake

Typo, Kentucky

I'd rather go to Typo
than Talcum or Dwarf.
They're in the Appalachians—
no Golden Gate, no Wharf.

Was it named for a mistake
made by flying fingers
switching *letetrs*, spelling
rong, signer instead of *singer*?

No. Research shows that Typo
is short for *Tie* and *Pole*.
That's how loggers fashioned rafts
to get their lumber sold.

They floated it to market
down Typo's rolling creek.
Could it be called Eraser?
I'll let you know next week.

—*George Ella Lyon*

Fayetteville
as in Fate

When I moved to Fayetteville, Arkansas
I soon learned to say it Fay'tteville, as in fate
I came into town the American way,
the immigrant way, the upwardly mobile
bedouin trekking across the highway
I moved here from New Jersey and I like it just fine,
although I miss belligerent store clerks
and being able to rent *Abi Fawq el-Shagara*
at the Egyptian video/ pizzeria/ travel agency/
check cashing service/ grocery store

It is Fay'tteville as in fate:
There is Cherokee and Choctaw in it
There is Spain and France left in the names of things
There is Wild West and Old South here
Sometimes the music of the Ozarks
spills down the mountainside
and it is green and brown, and I think I hear it

—*Mohja Kahf*

Grandma's **Front Porch**

The night sky alive with staccato stars,
the music homemade as blackberry pie.
A washboard rhythm, a six-string guitar,
and Grandpa on banjo. The still air fills
with sweet gospel hymns and songs from the hills.
Didn't It Rain and *Gentle Fair Jenny*,
This Train and *Go Tell It On the Mountain*.
Grandpa pulls the melody from the strings
like he's lighting the stars with his fingers—
bright, clear notes far too many for countin'.

—Eric Ode

Louisiana
Bayou
Song

Sometimes on the bayou in Louisiana
a storm rolls in quickly—
cypress trees
sway to the sound.

Sometimes on a quiet day
when the sun is high and hot
a heron happens by—
the bayou slows to the beat of his wading.

The song of the bayou
can be as fast and frenetic as a Zydeco two-step
or as soft and slow as a Cajun waltz—
the bayou sings a song to me.

—Margaret Simon

The Ninth Ward

Hurricane Katrina
New Orleans, Louisiana
August 29, 2005

Earlene Boudreau did not expect to die
The day the levees broke, but oh my Lord,
Her miracle went to a passer-by.

She heard the crackling bullhorn notify
Her help was on its way to the Ninth Ward.
Earlene Boudreau did not expect to die.

A helicopter did not hear the cry,
A girl strapped to a chimney by a cord.
Her miracle flew to a passer-by.

The water rose as much as nine feet high.
A flatboat came; she could not climb aboard.
Earlene Boudreau did not expect to die.

The government stuck to its alibi:
High cost of safety it could ill-afford.
Her miracle went to a passer-by.

The headline news: "A Nation Wonders Why
Katrina's Homeless Victims Are Ignored."
Earlene Boudreau did not expect to die:
Her miracle went to a passer-by.

—J. Patrick Lewis

Ella

Ella is to swing
What robin is to spring
What bee is to bee sting
The definition.

Ella is to big band
Like ocean is to sand
What glove is to a hand
A warm addition.

Ella is the fuse
To dynamite, the news
That poetry owes to muse—
Sheer inspiration

Ella is to class
Like energy to mass
What sunlight sends through glass
Illumination

—Mariel Bede

I Give Thanks for Trussville, Alabama

For the boxy blue house
on Lake Street

the low branch on the chinaberry tree,
perfect for spying

the rattle of the Red Flyer
as we pull it empty

across sidewalks cracked
and raised by the roots of ancient oaks.

For the library three blocks down
and one block over

where we build a soon-to-be
avalanche of books—

our wagon turned pumpkin
turned carriage turned train.

For the one stop light
blinking *caution   caution   caution*

for the noonday bus
wheezing its promise to carry us away—

someday,
but not until we're ready.

—*Irene Lathem*

Jesse Owens

He ran from dirt poor poverty
To fetch the gold that set him free.
He put Herr Hitler in his place
The day he won the human race.

—*Charles Ghigna*

OWENS (1913-1980) WON FOUR GOLD MEDALS
AT THE 1936 OLYMPICS IN GERMANY—
THE 100 AND 200 METERS, LONG JUMP, AND RELAY.

The Innocent

Emmett Till
1941–1955

Dark on that Mississippi Delta day,
My baby Emmett fell so far from grace
That Justice . . . What would Justice have to say?

They said a boy should never disobey.
They claimed he shamed a white girl to her face.
Dark on a Mississippi Delta day,

They beat him bloody, oh, they made him pay.
They kicked him, shot, and drowned him just in case—
And Justice could not find a word to say.

The killers were acquitted, by the way,
As Southern virtue gussied up in lace
Dark on a Mississippi Delta day.

They closed his casket, left it where it lay—
Seemed like to me it was a hiding place.
So Emmett's mama's justice had its say.

I laid my bloodied boy out on display.
But fifty thousand mourners won't erase
Dark from that Mississippi Delta day
When Justice did not have one word to say.

—*J. Patrick Lewis*

For **Trayvon Martin**

1995–2012

Instead of sleeping—
I walk with him from the store.
No Skittles, thank you.

We do not talk much—
Sneakers crossing the courtyard.
Humid Southern night.

We shake hands and hug—
Ancient, stoic tenderness.
I nod to the moon.

I'm so old school—
I hang till the latch clicks like
An unloaded gun.

—Reuben Jackson

Gator Theater

Step right on up and admire the gator!
Just look at the teeth in that mouth!
His strength is amazing. No creature is greater.
He's King of the Beasts in the South.

A masterful wrestler, a mountain of muscle
who's happy at home in the swamp,
he's fond of a fracas or free-for-all tussle.
He'll gratefully give you a chomp.

And here at our Florida roadside attraction,
we wrangle him into submission.
You'll witness displays of unparalleled action,
for only the price of admission.

You won't find a wilder, more spine-tingling show,
from South Carolina to Nome.
Just one word of caution we need you to know:
Please don't ever try this at home.

—Kenn Nesbitt

Foxtail Palm Ballet

Sway
        sashay
forth/back
        back/forth
        plié
command your landscape stage
dance
        a chassé
        a cambré
seize applause
take your bow
        encore
another jeté

for you are
a tropical showstopper
full-bodied
ballet

—*Lee Bennett Hopkins*

An American Wedding

Little Havana, Miami, Florida

Today my Cuban cousin married
a Colombian neighbor.

First we danced
the rumba and mambo,
then the cumbia,
and when Dominican neighbors
arrived, everyone started dancing
the merengue,
but soon an Argentine came,
so we danced the tango.

A Latino wedding in Miami
resembles the United Nations!

—Margarita Engle

Una Boda Americana

Hoy se casó mi prima cubana
con un vecino colombiano.

Primero bailamos
la rumba y el mambo,
después la cumbia,
y cuando llegaron los vecinos
dominicanos, todos se pusieron
a bailar el merengue,
pero pronto llegó un argentino,
y por eso bailamos el tango.

¡Una boda Latina en Miami
parece a las Naciones Unidas!

—_Translation by Margarita Engle_

Disney World

Orlando, Florida

Magic imprints every step
where dreams come true

Mosi, a Masai giraffe, grazes on
acacia leaves in Animal Kingdom.

Snow-capped Matterhorn shimmers
in simmering heat like a mirage.

Cinderella's tiered vanilla-wedding-cake
castle's spires prick a cerulean sky.

Pig-tailed girl with a pink Mickey hat
nibbles on a cloud of cotton candy.

Grumpy hugs a miniature Snow White,
red ribbon crooked in her hair, smiling for the camera.

Three kids clutching lap bars scream
plummeting past stars and comets in Space Mountain.

Fiery flowers explode—
oohs, ahhs

A boy, legs dangling over his father's shoulders,
nods off under a sleepy sky.

—Georgia Heard

Turkey Buzzard Time

In Ohio, everything turns festival—
corn, sauerkraut, lavender, pumpkins, pork.
What can we say?
Winter packs a trunk here, not an overnight bag—
a stubborn relative reluctant to leave
our golden rolling hills,
the rocky outcrops and caves
the undulating amber acres we love so.
But a festival answers it all—long winters,
loneliness, and the monotony of hard work.
Why, up in Hinckley even the homely Turkey Vulture
gets his own day, the Ides of March,
that maddening month
of mud and muck and snow.
Let's go, we'll get us a "buzzard burger"
and listen to a little bluegrass and that purdy ranger gal
go on about wingspans and migration
and how these cuss-ugly birds . . .
became the harbinger of spring!
Oh, it's something to do, I guess
until that next festival comes along.

—Tracie Vaughn

Valley View

Fair Play, Missouri, 1874

Church nearby, valley view,
Clear creek, a town grew.

A town grew, took a name—
Fair Play—the railroad came.

The railroad came—commercial coup,
Business flourished, Bill did too.

Bill Akard soon became
Star marksman, dead aim.

Dead aim, tried and true,
Countrywide folks all knew.

Folks all knew Bill Akard's fame.
Henry Starr arrived, they claim

Starr arrived, brought his crew
To rob the bank, pass on through.

Passed on through, called off his game
Due to Bill's crack shot acclaim.

To Bill's acclaim they bid adieu,
Headed east, away they flew.

Away they flew from what looked tame.
Fair Play went on the same.

Went on the same, the town that grew,
Church nearby, valley view.

—David L. Harrison

Poem to Be Read at **3** A.M.

Ladora, Iowa

Excepting the diner
On the outskirts
The town of Ladora
At 3 A.M.
Was dark but
For my headlights
And up in
One second-story room
A single light
Where someone
Was sick or
Perhaps reading
As I drove past
At seventy
Not thinking
This poem
Is for whoever
Had the light on

—Donald Justice

Willie Nelson

Songs are gifts, he says,
fallen straight out of the big blue sky,
caught on the strings of his
Martin guitar, scratched
in pencil on odd pieces of paper,
or in ink on the palm of his hand.
Doesn't matter.
Songs of faith, songs of loss,
songs of heartache and hotels,
and stars, lots of stars.

No matter where you go,
you'll hear it, a song by Willie
just winging along in the cool, cool air.
Maybe country, maybe jazz, maybe reggae,
maybe soul, each tune shot through with blues.
Go ahead, listen. Tap your toes. Hum along.
Soon enough, your own song might
fall out of the big blue sky.
Don't be surprised. Go ahead . . .
catch it. It's what Willie would do.

—Kathi Appelt

Ladies and Gentlemen—
The Ramones

hey ho let's go!
time to take back rock and roll
four sneering leather boys
in ripped up jeans
kicking out some jams
from a garage in Queens—
Joey, Johnny,
Dee Dee, and Tommy
punks before punk had a name
three chords and a cloud of dust
prove you don't have to be grown up
to earn a spot in the Hall of Fame

—Michael Salinger

Recipe for the First Derby Cars

The Soap Box Derby
Akron, Ohio

Begin
by simmering
the Great Depression
until you have a thick broth
of thrift and innovation.

Season
with memories—
snow, hill, sled, thrill—
just enough to whet
an appetite for speed.

Gather
camaraderie,
intuitive engineering,
scraps of wood and salvaged wheels,
ideas steeped in August heat.

—*Mary Lee Hahn*

The Place of 500 Miles

From backyards and porches,
in seats and in stands,
hundreds and hundreds of racing fans
look up to blue skies to chant a refrain :
  hold off the rain,
    just hold off the rain.

From legends and lore of past races won,
to gut and grit, to story and sun.

Where hopes have been shattered
and dreams have come true,
where race cars rumble into view . . .

as over fabled bricks they fly,
to crowd-roaring cheers beneath a May sky,
as legend and luck; magic and mirth
come together to watch
the greatest racing on Earth.

—*Rebecca Kai Dotlich*

Clothesline

Yields leftover line for jumpropes,
    frees small wooden men
      for handkerchief parachutes.

Supports cool, sheet-walled picnics
    of crackers and Kool-Aid.

Staggers, sometimes, under the load
    but recovers with the broomstick's help.

Admires the aim
    of robins and cowbirds.

Teaches patience to towels.

Lets the sun have its way,
    but makes the wind take
    the long way around.

Sends you running
    out into the rain.

—Diane Gilliam

Mt. Tom

Above the lake looms an Indiana dune,
Its bank of sand thrust down to the beach below,
Where whitecaps sculpture ripples night and noon.
The dune stands motionless against the flow.

Wind more than water sets its shaping fate.
So does a small boy clambering, his tow
Of hands and feet dimpling the great dune's weight.
The dune stands motionless against the blow.

And when the winter winds sweep off the lake
To chase the last of summer's afterglow,
They decorate a frosted angel cake,
The dune still motionless beneath the snow.

—L. M. Lewis

Grandpa Mails
the Sea to Ohio

Are you ready to smell the sea?
Mom unwraps a packet from Japan,
holds it open just under my nose
and pulls out a long crispy frond.

Are you ready to make the sea?
We soak the crinkled piece of seaweed
that Grandpa gathered, boiled, rinsed,
and hung to sun-dry on his beach.

Are you ready to taste the sea?
I lift the satin green wakame
from soup bowl to my mouth
and I savor—Grandpa's Sagami Sea.

—Holly Thompson

For an Island Wedding

Mackinac Island, Michigan

Once there was an inland sea,
its waters blue and beautiful
with absence, for there was nothing else
and this was once upon a time.

Out of this sea an island rose,
its conifers green with abundance,
its reaches white where the waves climbed,
and this was once upon a time.

Out of the island there rose a town,
its streets busy with men,
its harbor brown with boats
bearing the cargoes of the time.

Out of the town a church was raised,
its walls in all simplicity
contained like hands the faith
and the fervor of that time.

And out of this church that rose from the town
that rose from the island that rose from the sea
a man and woman came and joined.
Their love was green with abundance
and white where the waves climbed
and beautiful and blue. And it held like hands
in all simplicity our time,
and other times and once upon a time.

—John Barr

Great Lakes

Great Lakes
Against the river's mouths
The lake backs
Bunch back like the backs
Of a wolf pack
Their heads sunk in the sand
Their tails under the banks
All you see of them
Is what
They've turned to you—
Their backs—
While their wolf bellies drag the
Shallow fish paths
And brush by rusted hulls
Little people pit their edges
With buckets and blankets
Little people build their cities
And drain their sorrows into
Gitchi-gami
Mishigami
Karegnondi
Erielhonan
Onitariio
Out they go
Filling their hopes
In the rapids
In the narrows
Down the
Kaniatarowanenneh
Into the great
Gta'n

—JonArno Lawson

Sacred Land

Boundary Waters Canoe Area
Minnesota

Our silent canoe
glides endlessly through
pine, birch,
and blue spruce. Who knew
my seat to be a pew,
a perch,
with a timbered view
worshipped by so few?
My church.

—*Laura Purdie Salas*

Chicago, Tell Me Who You Are

I'm a city with a past, a memory
of wind-fed fire. No fear is like the fear
of a wooden city on a windy day.
Even the people were on fire. "Throw me in the river,"
a wife told her husband. "I'd rather drown than burn."

I'm Lincoln when he stands for President.
I'm the *City of Big Shoulders* and the World's Fair.
I'm Millennium Park and the long lakeshore,
the Magnificent Mile and tallest towers.
The Cubs and White Sox, Bulls and Bears.

My names are Baby Face, Capone, and Dillinger;
Sandburg, Gwen Brooks, Hemingway;
Disney, Orson Welles, and Tina Fey;
Oprah, Smashing Pumpkins, Nat King Cole;
Jack Benny, Belushi, and Steve Colbert.

I'm "Sunday in the Park" and George Seurat;
the Symphony of Reiner and Solti;
Sinatra and *Chicago, Chicago,*
they have the time, the time of their life.
I saw a man, he danced with his wife!

A floating line of lights, the world's planes
	converge on me.
Flaps extending, each one flowers as it lands.
Astronauts in space see something amazing:
a city rising from an inland sea.
My hands are filled with phosphorescent dreams.

—John Barr

O'Hare

Languages flit like hummingbirds
as passengers weave through
the terminal
their shoes small clues to the people inside them:
the CEO, confident in black polished pumps, clicks past
scrolling through details of her Detroit morning meeting
a student, shuffling by in scuffed chucks,
can almost taste his granny's chicken pot pie now that he's near,
an immigrant, sandals peeking out from a saffron silken sari,
scans the crowd for the sister she's missed every day for sixteen years.
This airport, like any, is a microcosm—
a smear on the slide of humanity's deepest desires:
connection
arrival
adventure

—Tracie Vaughn

The Chicago River

St. Patrick's Day

It is quite a sight, that it is
River churning, turning green
Leprechauns, to be sure
Men dump powder, that they do
But who gave the recipe?
Leprechauns, to be sure
 I will watch the parade, that I will
  Kilts and shamrocks
  Irish dancers
  Flag-flying floats
  Pipe and drum bands
But who tricked a river
Into thinking it's Irish?
Leprechauns, to be sure

—Donna Marie Merritt

At the Twinsburg Festival

Twinsburg, Ohio

She is the bloom on the rose.
She is the moon in the sky.
He is the sauce for the goose.
He is the thumb in the pie.

He is the key to the lock.
She is the glint on the gold.
He is the star in the night.
She is the warmth in the cold.

She is the singer of songs.
He is the get-up and go.
He is the flame in the fire.
She is the afterglow.

—Peter Kostin

Tulip Time Festival

Holland, Michigan

Tulips paint the city
in yellow, red, and white—
a canvas washed with petals,
brushed with morning light.
It's blooming time in Holland.

Dancers bloom in bonnets
with twirling skirts and stomps—
a field of wooden shoes,
a sweep of kicks and clomps.
It's klompen time in Holland.

Springtime skips to *klompen*
as bands parade the streets—
We wave to floats with tulips,
we savor Holland's treats!
It's Tulip Time in Holland!

—Buffy Silverman

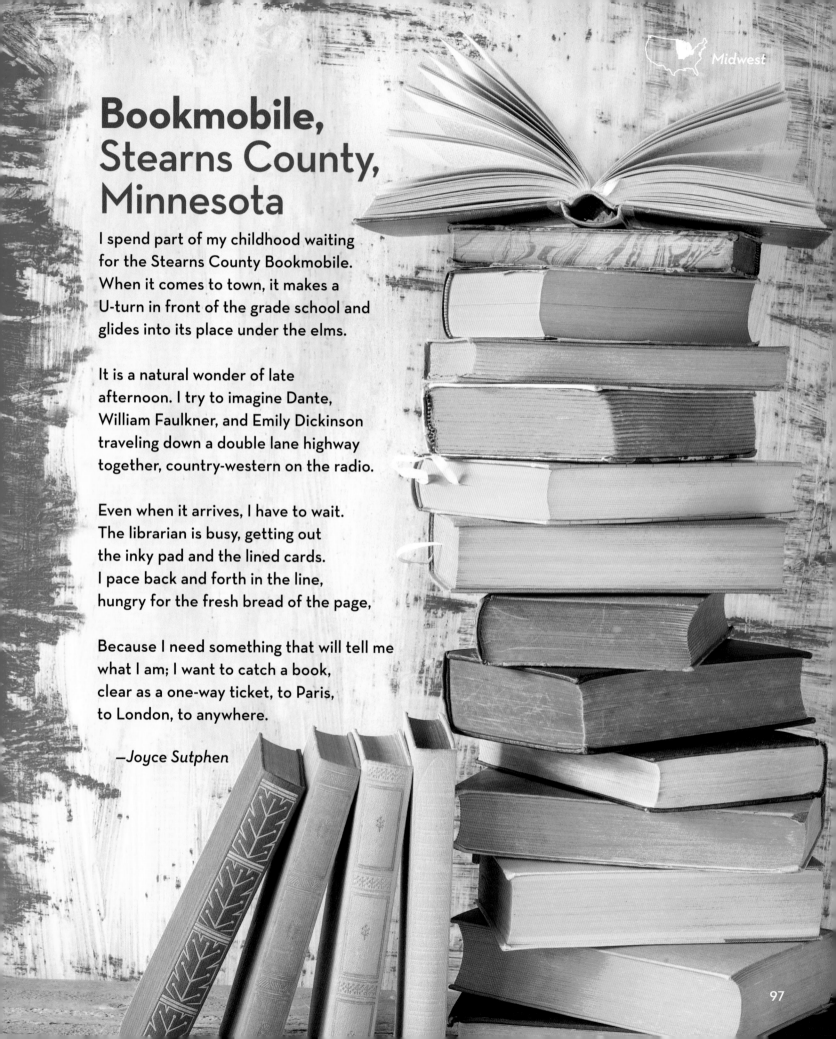

Bookmobile, Stearns County, Minnesota

I spend part of my childhood waiting
for the Stearns County Bookmobile.
When it comes to town, it makes a
U-turn in front of the grade school and
glides into its place under the elms.

It is a natural wonder of late
afternoon. I try to imagine Dante,
William Faulkner, and Emily Dickinson
traveling down a double lane highway
together, country-western on the radio.

Even when it arrives, I have to wait.
The librarian is busy, getting out
the inky pad and the lined cards.
I pace back and forth in the line,
hungry for the fresh bread of the page,

Because I need something that will tell me
what I am; I want to catch a book,
clear as a one-way ticket, to Paris,
to London, to anywhere.

—*Joyce Sutphen*

Three Girls on Skates

I look down into the viewfinder's gray
blur—this was when you didn't get what you
saw; this was in the days of black and white.

My friends, standing in the schoolyard, have their
woolen scarves tied tightly under the chin;
they have snow pants pulled over their dresses,

and their woolen coats come down to the knee,
but it's because of the skates, polished white,
that I took the picture, using the black

camera that must have come from somewhere,
from those indulgent parents I never
thanked, the same ones who flooded the playground

to make a place for us to skate. Who would
have thought life could ever have been so good?

—*Joyce Sutphen*

The Menorah

Most of the year, I sit and wait.
When the days grow cold and dark,
someone pulls me out.
I'm rubbed and shined,
old wax pried from my fists.
Voices tell the story of how I came here,
hidden in a suitcase, wrapped in a blanket.
At night I stand in the window, defying the dark.
Behind me, my family glows
with the light of my fire,
with the story of an ancient miracle,
with the joy of eating latkes, spinning dreidels,
singing, together, year after year.
Every night I am handed one more flame—
until my hands are full.
I savor the moment,
while I sit and wait, knowing
the cold, dark days will come again.

—*Elizabeth Steinglass*

Emmylou Oberkfell:
Fifth Grade Poem on America

America
is a
big
Christmas
pie:
the Middle West
is berries,
the rest
is
just
crust.

—*Dave Etter*

Turtle

Mrs. Kash, my math teacher,
tried to get me to take off
my backpack. I said I couldn't.
.

She said, "That's no way to sit
at a desk." "It's okay," I told her.
"It can't be comfortable," she said.

"But I need my stuff," I insisted.
She sent me to the counselor.
Ms. Greene asked if there was

anything I wanted to talk about.
I wanted to shout: Leave me alone!
But if I did, the next stop would be

the principal. So I shook my head.
"Can you tell me what's *in* that
backpack?" she asked. I shook

my head again. I wanted to crawl
way back in the cave of myself,
maybe go to sleep. "Where did

you sleep last night?" she asked.
Did she read my mind?
Her question made the walls

of the room close in. "Mason?"
she asked, leaning forward. "Are
you listening?" I hunted

for what to say, came up
with words from her
Stranger Danger talk. "Some

things are private," I said. She
sat back. "Where are you living?"
she asked. It was hard to breathe.

—George Ella Lyon

Give-Away

The book lady at the Salvation
Army read us a book that says
a book is a house. She liked it,
I could tell. She's got a house,
I bet, with lots of books in it.

Under the by-pass bridge where
we lived before we got here
and where we'll likely live again
when Daddy comes back because
this shelter is "women and children

only" and Daddy says our motto
is "together, no matter what,"
I don't think we could have
moved into a book. Still, when
the lady said we could take any
book we wanted, that's what I took.

—George Ella Lyon

The Poor

We see them keeping warm
Before and after storm
As prisoners to whom
The world assigns one room,
Its door and window cracks
Stoppered with burlap sacks—

We see them meanly holed
Up, rags all helter-skelter
In shells that aren't much shelter
At twenty-five below
Against the cleanly cold,
The glittering stars and snow.

—James Hayford

Cardamom Bread Topped with Walnuts

Mother is kneading dough spiced with cardamom.
The boy's work is walnuts.
Mother helps him spread them between dish towels
and use a hammer to break the shells.
He is picking the nutmeats out.
His whole life long, he'll remember the way the kitchen stool
rocked just a little under his feet, how his mother
knew exactly what to do, how the stormy Iowa sky
stayed on the other side of the glass.
This boy's father never forgot the thumping
of his mother's loom in a farmhouse cellar in Nebraska.
The boy's grandfather was once a boy in Sweden
whose mother pulled her spinning wheel a bit closer to the fire.
Then the sweet whirling sound
started again.

—*Susan Marie Swanson*

The Arabic Numbers
in America

The feast is ready for the Eid Celebration
And all the seats are taken.
So I stand on the hyphen of my new identity
of Arab-American
And lean on songs from Morocco,
Palestine and Lebanon.
Then suddenly I hear a knock on the door
and see the Arabic numbers arriving!
After the meal and over
cups of Arabic coffee and cardamom
I ask number one a question:
For centuries you have been a citizen everywhere
And you continue to remember your origin?!
He answers me with affection:
To count numbers means to know where you began
in addition to where you are going. . .
He teaches me lesson one
in the mathematics of immigration.

—*Ibtisam Barakat*

The Mississippi River

is
an   African   river.
Black American mud.
Black American t o e
             a n d
             t a p
             a n d
             song.

The   blues:
this black
      blues
       river
        flows
back
ward.

An African   river.
An African   people
in American   m u d:
            s i n g
               i n g
            s o m e
            h i g h e r
            g r o u n d
            s o n g.

—Arnold Adoff

104

Mitchi Sibo

Mississippi,
great river flowing
through the very heart of our nation,
you are the holder
of the drumbeat of thunder,
the keeper of the breath of rain.

Great River, Mitchi Sibo,
so Lenape guides
who showed the white men
the way down your waters,
called you more than
three centuries ago.

Since then engineers
have tried to control you.
Leveed and dammed,
poured concrete, piled stones.

Yet you still submerge
every human attempt
to keep you from your ancient course,
your rendezvous with living wetlands,
as you bring them the gifts of life.

—Joseph Bruchac

MARK TWAIN
1835-1910

Mr. Twain

Hannibal's Gift

Missouri kids give thanks for Mr. Twain
For telling them the tales of Tom and Huck.
He said his words were truthful in the main.

Tom and Huck could sometimes be a pain
But none would say they ever lacked for pluck.
Missouri kids give thanks for Mr. Twain.

For Tom to sit in classes was a strain.
Aunt Polly heard excuses with a cluck.
She hoped his words were truthful in the main.

Huck's drunken pappy was a bane
But Huck was quick and knew the time to duck.
Missouri kids give thanks for Mr. Twain.

Tom and Huck could never quite refrain
From trouble but they always got unstuck.
They swore their words were truthful in the main.

Children's authors dream that they'll attain
The Twain Award with writing skill and luck.
Everyone gives thanks for Mr. Twain.
Their words they say are truthful in the main.

—David L. Harrison

Suburbia

We live in suburbia.
We call it "the burbs."
Where grass is green,
And we grow herbs.
There are no sidewalks,
Only curbs.
And no one complains.
And no one disturbs.
And all of the children
Are handsome and pretty.
But when we get **BORED**
We go to the city.

—Douglas Florian

Living in the Center

For my father, and the American Midwest

He thought he could stretch his arms out and touch both sides.
East coast, west, both will be mine if I live in the middle.
Proud immigrant student, he chose Kansas, then Missouri.
Shining Mississippi River, thread that tied us north to south,
French-Canadians, Italians, farmers, my Arab daddy's silk necktie,
black and white kids, old houses with porches and pitched roofs,
O Ferguson, Missouri, no one ever heard of you,
unless they lived in Cool Valley or Florissant, but we all heard of
Mark Twain, traveling north to Hannibal to stand in his rooms,
and Eugene Field, poet of the south side who left his toys
when he grew up. We saw the Arch rise, that last silver chunk
swung into place with a massive crane and bet it could not stand.
"Gateway to the West" but we felt like "Gateway to Everywhere" –
lucky, centered, balanced between mountain ranges,
mixed and blended like the whole spirit of a nation that held us
in its most important pocket where a person keeps money or tissues
and is always poking a hand in to make sure it is still there.

—Naomi Shihab Nye

GREAT

PLAINS

Silence **in North Dakota**

Over the lip of the Killdeer Canyon
five hundred feet over the tan buttes
that flank the Little Missouri
in the middle of North Dakota
in the middle of North America
in the middle of the western hemisphere
on tax day in the middle of April
at almost the end of the second millennium
the universe held its breath
for a full minute.

Complete, inviolate silence—
not a crow cawed
not a frog croaked
the wind shut its mouth
the cars and tractors stopped
the TVs all went dead
words failed for no good reason
clouds scudded but kept quiet about it
and everything alive or
what is sometimes called not-alive
listened to everything else
stones, motors, crocuses, blood pulsing
And then the crow cawed,
(that seemed to be the signal)
and the universe exhaled
and everything started again
but for that minute we heard
what it was really like.
                    —*Bill Holm*

Outside Fargo,
North Dakota

Along the sprawled body of the derailed
Great Northern freight car,
I strike a match slowly and lift it slowly.
No wind.

Beyond town, three heavy white horses
Wade all the way to their shoulders
In a silo shadow.

Suddenly the freight car lurches.
The door slams back, a man with a flashlight
Calls me good evening.
I nod as I write good evening, lonely
And sick for home.

—James Wright

I See the **Campanile**
Brookings, South Dakota

After a picnic at Oakwood Park,
a campfire, singing, a marshmallow roast,
we're all in the car driving through the dark
across the prairie, going home. Who is the most
wide-awake among us? Who will be first to spot
the campanile rising into the sky
as we drive into Brookings tonight? I've got
good eyes, we've done this before—I
know exactly where to look. I keep
my eyes on the road ahead—around the next bend—
there! See the tall tower flashing its light?
My brothers and sisters have fallen asleep,
so I'm the first to chant: *I see the campanile!* At the end
of a perfect day, it guides us home through the night.

—Helen Frost

So This Is **Nebraska**

The gravel road rides with a slow gallop
over the fields, the telephone lines
streaming behind, its billow of dust
full of the sparks of redwing blackbirds.

On either side, those dear old ladies,
the loosening barns, their little windows
dulled by cataracts of hay and cobwebs
hide broken tractors under their skirts.

So this is Nebraska. A Sunday
afternoon; July. Driving along
with your hand out squeezing the air,
a meadowlark waiting on every post.

Behind a shelterbelt of cedars,
top-deep in hollyhocks, pollen and bees,
a pickup kicks its fenders off
and settles back to read the clouds.

You feel like that; you feel like letting
your tires go flat, like letting the mice
build a nest in your muffler, like being
no more than a truck in the weeds,

clucking with chickens or sticky with honey
or holding a skinny old man in your lap
while he watches the road, waiting
for someone to wave to. You feel like

waving. You feel like stopping the car
and dancing around on the road. You wave
instead and leave your hand out gliding
larklike over the wheat, over the houses.

—Ted Kooser

Red **Convertible,**
1965

"Wouldn't that be interesting!"
Grama yelled, as we blew past abandoned farms
on a baking black two-lane road
in my mother's new red Cougar convertible.

Grama had to ride in front
on account of having just had her hair done,
but my mother didn't care:

her black hair
flew about her face
in slow-motion.
She'd bought new sunglasses for the trip
to match the red upholstery.

The wild map bucked
in Grama's hands
and I foresaw the consequences of it
getting away:
all of us doomed to be lost in a strange state
without a man.

I gripped my sister's hand and
together we hunched down in the back seat
out of the wind.
"Can we put the top back up?" we cried.

My mother sighed.

—Darrah Cloud

Mount Rushmore

Gutzon Borglum designed four faces
to gaze across the western skyline.
Four hundred miners built roads,
blasted stone, sharpened drill bits,
ran the hoists, and generated power.

Norman "Happy" Anderson, a skilled
powderman, earned $1.25 an hour,
more than mines were paying at the time.
Happy's dynamite words may have
chiseled for him a bonus:

I put the curl in Lincoln's beard,
the part in Teddy's hair,
and the twinkle in Washington's eye.

—Peter Kostin

The Black Hills

The Paha Sapa,
the ancient Black Hills,
hold the center of the world.

So the old people say,
just as Black Elk did.

Though others claimed them
with pieces of paper,
the Lakotas know it
the other way round.

The Black Hills remain the place
that reaches for them
the way a mother holds out
her arms for her children.

Seen from a distance,
those hills look like shadows
but as you approach them
they fill with light,
the bright green of the pines,
the white fire of sacred sage,
the glow of remembering rocks
that hold more worth
than the gold white men
killed and died for.

The wind that flows
out of the hills
is still the breath
of the Great Mystery.

The Black Hills remain
part of the people,
the place that remembers,
the place to pray.

—Joseph Bruchac

Omaha

Red barns and red heifers spot the green
grass circles around Omaha—the farmers
haul tanks of cream and wagonloads of
cheese.

Shale hogbacks across the river at Council
Bluffs—and shanties hang by an eyelash to
the hill slants back around Omaha.

A span of steel ties up the kin of Iowa and
Nebraska across the yellow, big-hoofed Missouri
River.

Omaha, the roughneck, feeds armies,
Eats and swears from a dirty face.
Omaha works to get the world a breakfast.

—*Carl Sandburg*

Farm Workers
on the Fields

On the fields
at a distance
among the green of lettuce, spinach,
broccoli, watermelon, cantaloupe,
they look like flowers.

As we approach
we see the colors are bright shirts
on the bent backs of migrant
farm workers on the fields.

Unprotected
from harm of pesticides and fertilizers,
poorly paid,
they plant, weed, gather
the best foods for our nourishing,
earning mere sustenance for their families,
all profit for the growers
until the dream of justice,
a dream for long by so many,
is achieved
on the fields.

—*Alma Flor Ada*

117

Where is the Fourth of July?

The Fourth of July
  isn't what it used to be,
    isn't what it used to be,
      not even close to being close
       to what it used to be
        back in the days of old.

Where is the Fourth of July parade?
  The bands? Remember the bands that played,
    picnics, cookouts, firework adventures?
      Remember when Grandpa lost his dentures,
       Granny made ice cream, the four uncles sang
        (almost in tune) like a barbershop gang,

Saluting the flag dressed in red, white, and blue?
  Kids riding bikes down the avenue?
    Where is the Fourth of July of old?
      I said to Gramps, "It's holiday gold!
       July the Fourth is a household word!"
        But missing his teeth, he said to me, "Son,
      Ish only July da fird."

                 —*Anonymous*

April Fool's Day

They say you're the picture of pretty,
You're as warm as the heat from the sun,
You're the lock and the key to the city,
You're the meat in a hamburger bun!

They say you're the pick of the litter,
They say that you're such a good egg
But, kid, have you stopped to consider
Someone might be pulling your leg?!

              —*Peter Kostin*

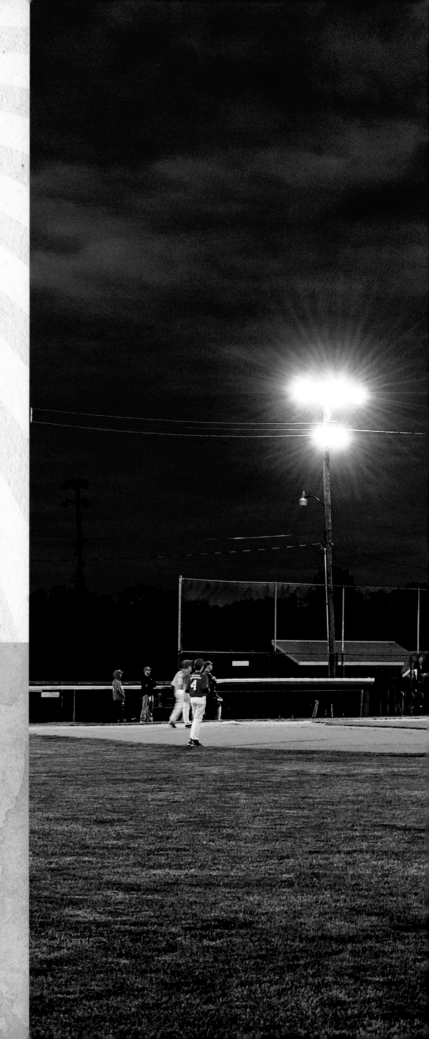

Little League Night Game

Beneath a sinking summer sky,
I hear my parents cheering.
I lift my heavy bat and know
my time for truth is nearing.

The scent of hope and hot dogs
is mixed with grass and dirt.
My heart is doing somersaults
beneath my sticky shirt.

I stride into the batter's box
and take a cut or two.
My butterflies are well disguised
inside my follow-through.

Two strikes fly by, then I connect
and launch a shot to right.
It seems my heart has joined the ball
that's arcing through the night.

With feet on first, I sense at last
my star is on the move.
As my team's only girl, I know
I've got a lot to prove.

—Ted Scheu

Child's Chant

Oklahoma Dust Bowl, 1935

Dust blows in, dust blows out.
Drought brings dust, dust brings drought.
Right hand in, swirl about—
dust blows in, dust blows out.

Bury scarecrow, bury cow,
bury chickens, bury plow.
Dust blows in, dust blows out—
left hand in, swirl about.

Papa fiddles, baby cries,
Mama stares at empty skies.
Right foot in, swirl about—
dust blows in, dust blows out.

Dust for breakfast, dust for dinner.
Crops stop growing, hope grows thinner.
Dust blows in, dust blows out—
left foot in, swirl about.

Packed jalopy, laden mule.
Goodbye friends, goodbye school.
Whole self in, swirl about—
dust blows in; we blow out.

—Renée M. LaTulippe

Tumbleweed

The tumbleweed shows
that some things travel
after they die
Withered, dry
it crisscrosses the plains
passing by
watchful pronghorns
catching a sleepy buffalo's eye
The tumbleweed knows
that some things live
after they die
Strangely spry
it scatters scores of seeds
that softly lie
in wait for rain
and a brief toehold in the earth
before they say good-bye

—Marilyn Singer

Teddy Roosevelt in Medora

Medora, North Dakota

In the old Dakota badlands
where a Marquis chose to settle
came a young man from Manhattan
with an urge to test his mettle.

He had money, he had comfort,
and a spacious, lovely home,
but he left it all behind him
for the buttes where bison roam.

In the years to come, as president,
the world's most famous man,
would declare, "It's in Medora
where my life's romance began."

—Robert Schechter

Buffalo Commons

In Antler, Reeder,
Ryder and Streeter,
stray dogs bristle
when strangers pass.

In Brocket, Braddock,
Maddock and Wheelock
dry winds whistle
through broken glass.

The steeples are toppled
and the land unpeopled,
reclaimed by thistle
and buffalo grass.

—Timothy Murphy

BUFFALO COMMONS IS A VAST NATURE RESERVE PROPOSED FOR THE GREAT PLAINS, WHICH WOULD REINTRODUCE THE AMERICAN BUFFALO.

Stories from Kansas

Little bunches of
grass pretend they are bushes
that will never bow.
    They bow.

Carelessly the earth
escapes, loping out from the
timid little towns
    toward Colorado.

Which of the horses
we passed yesterday whinnied
all night in my dreams?
    I want that one.

    —William Stafford

A Place in **Kansas**

For Jon Gierlich

Somewhere in Kansas, a friend found
An empty stone house alone in a wheatfield.
Over the door was incised a ship's anchor.
There was no one to ask
What that anchor was doing in Kansas,
No water for miles.
Not a single white sail of meaning
Broke the horizon, though he stood there for hours.
It's like that in Kansas, forever.

—*Ted Kooser*

Crossing Kansas **By Train**

The telephone poles
have been holding their
arms out
a long time now
to birds
that will not
settle there
but pass with
strange cawings
westward to
where dark trees
gather about
a waterhole. This
is Kansas. The
mountains start here
just behind
the closed eyes
of a farmer's
sons asleep
in their workclothes.

—*Donald Justice*

School Buses

You'd think that by the end of June they'd take themselves
Away, get out of sight—but no, they don't; they
Don't at all. You see them waiting through
July in clumps of sumac near the railroad, or
Behind a service station, watching, always watching for a
Child who's let go of summer's hand and strayed. I have
Seen them hunting on the roads of August—empty buses
Scanning woods and ponds with rows of empty eyes. This
  morning
I saw five of them, parked like a week of
Schooldays, smiling slow in orange paint and
Smirking with their mirrors in the sun—
But summer isn't done! Not yet!

—Russell Hoban

The World's Largest Ball of Twine

in memory of Frank Stoeber

In Cawker City, Kansas, in the distant long-ago,
a simple farmer had a simple dream
to make the largest ball of twine the world would ever know,
the likes of which no one had ever seen.

And through the winding years that ball of twine increased in size
around the simple dream it held inside.
But then, one day, the simple farmer simply closed his eyes.
He wound one final strand, and then he died.

Now once a year the Cawker City citizens unite
to tend the dream the farmer left behind.
And as their hopeful hands keep winding late into the night,
dreams present, past, and future intertwine.

—Allan Wolf

BESSIE COLEMAN
1892–1926

Bessie
and
Amelia

Bessie Coleman: risk-taker.
Barnstorming daredevil whose stunts
lifted brown faces to the sky,
elevated dreams that soared without limits.

Amelia Earhart: record-breaker.
Insatiable hunger for
highest, fastest, solo, nonstop
launched dreams that soared without limits.

Bessie and Amelia: trend-setters.
All-American aviatrixes who
overcame barriers of race and gender,
lived their dreams, soared despite limits.

—Mary Lee Hahn

AMELIA EARHART
1897–1937

125

La luz de **El Paso**

Cuando el sol sale en la quietud de la mañana,
en lo que hace millones de años fuese un antiguo mar,
en el inhóspito desierto de Chihuahua, en el oriente tejano,
corre el Río Bravo

entre El Paso y Juárez, ciudades fronterizas, ciudades hermanas;
El Paso, en tierra antes española,
y luego mexicana, nuevo mexicana y, en 1850, texana.

Todos los días, los paseños pueden ver otro país
que lucha por la justica así como todos los países luchan,
su música, arte, mercados, demasiados niños hambrientos.

Las familias de El Paso escuchan inglés y español, disfrutan
el acogedor aroma de la lluvia, el desierto, sus lagartijas, fósiles,
cactos; sus valles en las afueras de la ciudad donde un halcón vuela
sobre campos de algodón, caballos, canales de riego.

Una ciudad de grandiosas puestas de sol dorado y naranja sobre las mesas.

Una estrella blanca hecha de luces brilla en el Monte Franklin
y en Navidad, las luminarias resplandecen en las frías
calles de los barrios. Las familias se reúnen para compartir risa, abrazos,
tamales, galletas navideñas; luces navideñas, estrellas relucientes.

El Paso: aún en el frío del desierto, una ciudad de sonrisas cálidas.

—Translation by Dr. Gabriela Baeza Ventura

El Paso's Light

As the sun rises in the morning quiet,
in what millions of years ago was an old sea,
in the stark Chihuahua desert, at the west tip of Texas,
the Rio Grande flows

between El Paso and Juárez, border cities, sister cities;
El Paso, *the pass* in Spanish, once native land,
then Mexico, New Mexico and in 1850, Texas.

Every day, El Pasoans can see another country
with its struggles for justice as all countries struggle,
its music, art, markets, too many hungry children.

El Paso families hear English and Spanish, enjoy
rain's welcome scent, the desert, its lizards, fossils,
cactus; its valleys on the edges of town where a hawk flies
above fields of cotton, horses, irrigation canals.

A city of grand gold and orange sunsets on the mesas.

A white star made of lights shines on Mount Franklin,
and at Christmas, luminarias glow on chilly
neighborhood streets. Families gather for laughter, hugs,
tamales, Christmas cookies; holiday lights, glittering stars.

El Paso: even in the desert cold, a city of warm smiles.

—*Pat Mora*

Great Plains

Old Vogal

Told me I was lucky
When I went to cut his hay
A bloom or two means lots of leaves
'Course it's best that way.

He assured me I was lucky
That my bales were done up tight
Lucky that I caught the dew
And chanced to bale it right.

Oh yes, and I was lucky
When the storm clouds came around
All my hay was in a stack
Not layin' on the ground.

I clenched my jaw and held my tongue
Red anger 'round me swirled
If I was a man, he'd say I was good.
But "lucky" 'cuz I'm a girl.

—*Peggy Godfrey*

Marion Mitchell Morrison

Born big at 13 pounds, he grew straight
as a Douglas Fir and just about as tall.
Nicknamed "Little Duke" he played football
until a broken bone that wouldn't set
cost him his scholarship at USC.

Worked as a prop boy on sets in Hollywood.
Played extras, got a bit part, then got more:
singing cowboy, horse operas by the score.
Did his own stunts, learned to shoot and ride
as Union cavalry or D-Day infantry.

Perfected the walk, the squint, the hesitant drawl
that meant, "I'm not looking for trouble but
as soon would throw a bottle at your head as not."
"Talk low," he said, "Talk slow. Or, better, not at all."
He never had to assert his masculinity.

The words he would like to be remembered by:
"Feo fuerte y formal," by which the Mexicans mean,
"He was ugly, strong and had dignity."
Even his critics agreed, the man on screen
and the man you met were one and the same John Wayne.

—*John Barr*

JOHN WAYNE
1907–1979

At the Drive-In

Papa says, *settle down,*
and Mama hands us

brown paper bags
of home-popped popcorn

as movie-music trickles
from the car speakers

and the giant screen
flickers alive.

My eyes move up
      and up

to the starstruck,
wide-as-forever sky

as cricketsong rises
from the evergreens,

and each time we go

it's the best movie
I've ever seen.

—*Irene Lathem*

That Day

President Kennedy's Assassination
November 22, 1963
Dallas, Texas

At her punch press.
Behind his counter.
Sitting in their desks.
Driving truck.
Watching a soap opera.
All programs interrupted.
It was after lunch when they heard—
A scratchy loud speaker.
A phone call.
A radio alert.
A newscaster in tears.
Open mouths were covered.
Eyes burned.
Hearts clutched.
A nation of people gathered to watch.
Dallas. An open limousine.
Her pink suit in black and white.
A screaming ambulance.
A gray tornado of images,
then somber silence.
Our President is dead.

—*Sara Holbrook*

THE JOHN F. KENNEDY ETERNAL FLAME WAS
PERMANENTLY ESTABLISHED IN 1967.

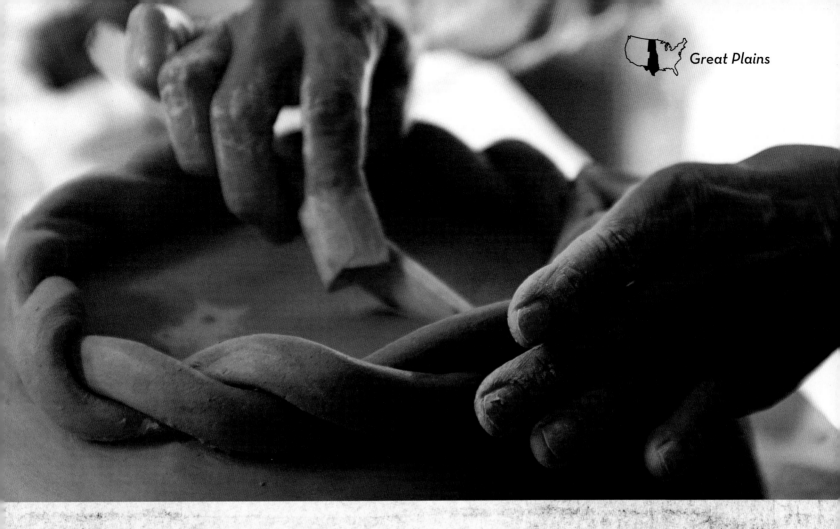

Yet To Be Told

**for the clay artists of MujerArtes,
San Antonio, Texas**

San Cuilmas, San Quilmas, San Anto, mi Santo.
We have not forgotten our names. They are
carved into old stone and hum in the newest
tunes. They shout from the glint of the slow-
moving low rider's soap bubble finish, are baked
into tiny clay trees, streets, churches and cafés
shaped by women entwined with the barrio's
thickest root, women who've rescued an art
folk thought long lost, taught themselves
how to tell time with earth and water,
how days pass on this side of the wild river.
San Cuilmas, San Quilmas, San Anto, mi Santo,
an air crowded with story after story.

—Rosemary Catacalos

Aún por contar

**para las artesanas de MujerArtes,
San Antonio, Texas**

San Cuilmas, San Quilmas, San Anto, mi Santo.
No hemos olvidado nuestros nombres. Están
grabados en piedra vieja, canturrean en las más
nuevas melodías. Gritan desde el brillo del
carrucho piel de burbuja, están inscritos en barro,
en ramitas, callecitas, Iglesias y fonditas creadas
por mujeres enlazadas con la raíz mas gruesa
del barrio, mujeres que han recuperado
una artesanía que habíamos dado por perdida,
autodidactas en medir el tiempo con agua y tierra,
en cómo pasan los días de éste lado del río.
San Cuilmas, San Quilmas, San Anto, mi Santo,
un aire abarrotado de historia tras historia.

—Translation by Rosemary Catacalos

First Men on the Moon

"The Eagle has landed!"
Apollo 11 Commander Neil A. Armstrong

"A magnificent desolation!"
Air Force Colonel Edwin F. "Buzz" Aldrin, Jr.
July 20, 1969

That afternoon in mid-July,
Two pilgrims watched from distant space
The Moon ballooning in the sky.
They rose to meet it face-to-face.

Their spidery spaceship *Eagle* dropped
Down gently on the lunar sand.
And when the module's engines stopped,
Cold silence fell across the land.

The first man down the ladder, Neil,
Spoke words that we remember now—
"Small step for man..." It made us feel
As if we too were there somehow.

Then Neil planted the flag and Buzz
Collected lunar rocks and dust.
They hopped like kangaroos because
Of gravity. Or wanderlust.

A quarter million miles away,
One small blue planet watched in awe.
And no one who was there that day
Will soon forget the Moon they saw.

—J. Patrick Lewis

Chandra

On July 23, 1999, Space Shuttle Columbia
carried into space NASA's Chandra X-ray Observatory,
which is named for Subrahmanyan
Chandrasekhar (1910–1995), winner of the
1983 Nobel Prize for Physics.

X-rays strike nested mirrors.
Orbiting telescope turns invisible light into data,
into pictures: exploded stars, colliding galaxies,
the edges of a supermassive black hole
at the heart of our own Milky Way.

Flagship American space observatory,
named for an Indian genius.

Think of him in the last century. Young Chandra,
on the deck of an ocean liner, dazzled by starlight
on the water, scribbling equations in a notebook.

How are stars born? How do they age and die?
A wondering mind from long ago leads us now to map
the substance of stars, the dances of galaxies.

—Uma Krishnaswami

ROCKY

MOUNTAIN

WEST

Annual Hog-Calling Contest

Montana State Fair
Billings, Montana

Farmwork is hard work; we rise with the sun.
But fair time is our time to take in some fun.

We clean up and preen up—our blue-ribbon best.
The folks that we meet there are mighty impressed.

We gawk at the midway and hoopla of lights.
But mostly we treasure the sillier sights.

The best is the hog-calling contest, for sure.
It's crowded and loud—all-American pure.

The grunting and "sooey-ing" aimed at the swine
just tickle my trotters and tingle my spine.

If only they knew what we porkers all know—
their calls hardly work, but we sure love the show.

—Ted Scheu

Anything for a **Buck**

Rodeo Cowboy, you're rugged and tough,
but riding a hurricane's gonna be rough.
Fans whistle and cheer as the gate is released—
You explode from the chute on a wild-eyed beast.

The ornery bronco's a reckless back-bender.
He whips you around like you're ice in a blender.
You can't lose your nerve or your one-handed grip
as you spin like a pinwheel and pitch like a ship.

A cyclone with hooves, he's a thrashing machine.
The crowd's on its feet. Hear 'em holler and scream.
Cling to the devil! Fire burns in his belly.
His jackhammer bucks turn your bones into jelly.

Like a crash-testing dummy, you snap back and forth.
You're jettisoned off with cen-*trif*-ugal force.
A five-second ride, then your duff hits the dirt.
Luckily, only your pride has been hurt.

You dust yourself off. Every joint seems to ache.
But it's part of the job that cowboys undertake.
You live for the challenge, the duel, the dance . . .
And you'll ride every time that you're given the chance.

—*Heidi Bee Roemer*

The Jackalope

Douglas, Wyoming

The oddest thing you've never seen
are antlered hares. They're very mean,
or so you'll hear if you pop in
to Douglas diners now and then.

A cry is heard up in the hills,
the kind of cry that gives you chills.
"The jackalope," townsfolk explain—
but if you look, you'll look in vain,

For no one's ever seen up close
that warrior rabbit. No one knows
just where it sleeps, how fierce its fight,
how high it leaps, how sharp its bite.

Indeed, this creature's very rare:
The only actual antlered hare
is mounted on a wall—a prop
made by a taxidermy shop.

Some taxidermists thought it fun
to sew two creatures into one—
but still at night it gives you chills
when lonely cries rise from those hills.

—Abigail Carroll

The Continental Divide

Yellowstone National Park

Along the crest of a wriggling trail
that winds and wends through Yellowstone Park,
you can straddle the Great Divide,
the ridge atop the country's "roof."

Whatever falls to your right—
raindrops, hail, snow, or—oops,
your bottled water—eventually
finds its way to the Atlantic.

And whatever falls to your left
seeps, trickles, sinks, or loops
toward the other ocean, the Pacific.
This country's split in watery sections:

every drip knows its directions.

—Michael J. Rosen

Sweat Lodge at the Gathering of Nations

Albuquerque, New Mexico

Within the sweat lodge covered by canvas
all is dark except for the glow of lava stones
piled within the pit in the center like pieces of Sun.

Those from every part of Turtle Island have come
to this gathering of nations, so within this lodge
there are two languages we all can speak.
One of them is English but the older tongue
is that of the heart and the drum beat.

For three days we will dance, sing songs
tell stories, and share the best of our cultures
with smiles on our faces and with pride
as emcees crack jokes about eating fry bread
and a new Miss Indian America is crowned.

But for now, to prepare in this sacred place
we pray for the healing of all who suffer,
to cleanse ourselves of twisted thoughts
and as the stones hiss and sweet steam rises
we give thanks for the greatest gift of all
that our children may see a new day.

—Joseph Bruchac

"Where There Is Water"

Keresan Pueblo, New Mexico

Mother dressed me as a boy
"To avoid problems during the journey."
Dad's pack looks heavy, he holds my hand.
There is a long road ahead.
We must be vigilant,
thieves are more dangerous than animals.
Divided in groups to walk faster
I hear them talk: north, better lands,
good work, a future.

We've been walking—a thousand miles,
it seems. At dawn we hear water running
downstream. We are thirsty.
As we approach the river, my father
pulls me to the ground. People from the pueblo
are filling their water jars.
They see us. Smiling they point to the stream:
"pe'kush" they say. "Pecos" says my father,
"Where there is water."
The Keresan pueblo is welcoming us.
Today is July 15th, 1541.

—F. Isabel Campoy

Legends of the Sonoran Desert

My mom left Tucson twice in her life.
Both times she came back fast and said,
"I like it better here."

She lets tarantulas walk up her arm. She says
all the collared lizard needs is a tie
and he can go to dinner anywhere.

She favors saguaro and chaparral. She blows
kisses at the unlovely javelina but she adores

the remorseless gila monster because,
"It looks like a fancy beaded purse your father
almost bought me."

—Ron Koertge

The **Bean Eaters**

They eat beans mostly, this old yellow pair.
Dinner is a casual affair.
Plain chipware on a plain and creaking wood,
Tin flatware.

Two who are Mostly Good.
Two who have lived their day,
But keep on putting on their clothes
And putting things away.

And remembering ...
Remembering, with twinklings and twinges,
As they lean over the beans in their rented back room that is full of beads and receipts and dolls and
cloths, tobacco crumbs, vases and fringes.

—*Gwendolyn Brooks*

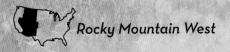
Backyard Barbecue

Local folk with local fare
gather in the summer where
everybody pitches in
to build a feast for kith and kin.

Kids with dogs help get set up—
tables, benches, napkins, cups—
then drift and scatter left and right
to go work up an appetite.

Mothers, who are organized,
chop, pare, peel, and caramelize.
Dads swap stories while they cook
flaky red July Chinook.

Around the table, bless and pass it!
Bannock fry bread in a basket!
Heaps of coleslaw, pots of beans!
Salsa made from nectarines!

Willpower! You have to try
to save room for the slabs of pie—
a yummy summit culinary:
luscious, juicy huckleberry.

—Susan Blackaby

Thanksgiving
In America

Pie Town, New Mexico

Down Rte. 60 on the continental divide
a town of dried up dreams now rolls out crust.
President Roosevelt sent Russell Lee
and his camera to capture the plight of Pie Town
in 1939—same year he created the national holiday.

Famous shots of dust-bowlers
at their church sings
trying to farm without water,
dancing among the ruins
of the Anasazi and Acoma.

It was the same dream out west
as in 1621 Plymouth,
but what happens when
the first settlers aren't first?

For some the fourth Thursday of November
represents a National Day of Mourning
not a day of unity, charity, and turkey.

Yet despite the great division of plates,
something blends people in Pie Town.
It doesn't matter whether you come
from the East or South or were born here,
at the Daily Pie they'll serve you a slice
of New Mexican Apple, granny smith
laced with green chili and piñon nuts.

—Stephanie Hemphill

143

A Rocky Mountain **Theology**

The god is dreaming of his birth,
how he sprang whole from fire and earth,
Laird Plain to Santa Fe,
his veins running rich with silver, lead, and gold.
He is a range of contradiction, young and old.
The panther, the wolf and the bighorn play
on his boulder-pocked and pine-scented skin,
and in winter, black and brown bears burrow in
his open pores, like mice in hay.
Moving but unmoved, he is indifferent to all human veneration—
activity, plans, conflict, conversation.
I scale his sacred vertebrae
and feel shaken, small, that is to say, awed
that some greater, even more perplexing god
has conceived, then spawned such fierce and pagan majesty.

—David Elliott

River at
Sunset

How bold is River!
Once again,
he has stolen
from Sun—

and is running swiftly,
carrying her golden
treasure on his back.

—*Kristine O'Connell George*

Fly Fisherman

He has walked into the river.

That's the first thing you think.
Any sane soul would pause
at the water's edge

but he walks into the river
wearing high-hipped boots
casting out
         and back
out
         and back
trying to lay the fly
                  lightly
      on the surface.

Standing in that restless water
he fishes for tranquility
and catches it each time
he drops the fly
ever-so-lightly
    on the river's glistening back.

—Ralph Fletcher

Colorado River Rapids

Eight to a raft,
Weighted with gear,
Life vests and helmets,
Guided by fear,
We're paddling westward
As whitewaters clash
Like molten lavas
Clouded in ash.

Canyons around us,
We're riding a sled
Past yellowed escarpments
Speckled with red.
Completing the picture,
The river below
Runs to a tundra
Of Vesuvian snow.

—Steven Withrow

Mass Ascension

at the Albuquerque International Balloon Fiesta

Wave upon
wave, they rise. A tide of
balloons in *folklórico* color, as
far as the eye can see. *Come on up,*
they say, *the air is cool and crisp as
desert champagne,* while thousands
below, *una familia internacional,*
stare up from a field, dewy-
green like chile,
and fall
   u   r
    n e
     d

New Mex-
ico's spell.

—*Michelle Heidenrich Barnes*

Broken Braid at Little Bighorn

Crow Agency, Montana

Like sacred sweetgrass

sadness grows up
from this wide plain
under one sky.

Here troops shed blood
to clear
the path to gold.

Here Crow shed blood
to save
their native ways.

Here Sioux shed blood
to shield
their independence.

Little Bighorn: a little river,
a little battle,
a bigger matter.

Little Bighorn: a little moment,
a last stand,
the beginning of the end.

Let sweetgrass be rebraided.

—Heidi Mordhorst

Once in the 40's

We were alone one night on a long
road in Montana. This was in winter, a big
night, far to the stars. We had hitched,
my wife and I, and left our ride at
a crossing to go on. Tired and cold—but
brave—we trudged along. This, we said,
was our life, watched over, allowed to go
where we wanted. We said we'd come back some time
when we got rich. We'd leave the others and find
a night like this, whatever we had to give,
and no matter how far, to be so happy again.

—William Stafford

148

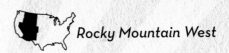
Twelfth Song
of **Thunder**

The voice that beautifies the land!
The voice above,
The voice of thunder
Within the dark cloud
Again and again it sounds,
The voice that beautifies the land.

The voice that beautifies the land!
The voice below,
The voice of the grasshopper
Among the plants
Again and again it sounds,
The voice that beautifies the land.

—*Anonymous (Navajo Tradition)*

149

Revenge

My gritty surface fosters speed,
plays right into your human need
to outwit physics, to be freed
from time's constraints.
You roar, you spin, you flame, you bleed.
I've no complaints,

for in between your harsh assaults,
your thieving from my salty vaults,
my vast, white, crusty soul exalts.
When you break through
my skin, your conquest swiftly halts:
I capture *you*.

—*Laura Purdie Salas*

BONNEVILLE SALT FLATS, UTAH

LAS VEGAS, NEVADA

Fan Favorites

Today's "Gravedigger" is haunting, it's true.
If you're in the finals, it's coming for you.
With green and black flames, a scary motif,
it'll bury the rich man, the beggar and thief.

"El Toro Loco," a five-ton beast,
is raging and cagy, to say the least.
In the freestyle final, it's got some pull.
But watch out, brother, for that crazy bull.

With "Scooby-Doo," there's a constant threat.
Can it run with the big dogs? Yeah, you bet!
It's driven by a lady with a bark and a bite.
When Scooby's in the finals, it's a big dog fight.

—Ken Slesarik

Stratosphere Casino, Hotel, and Tower

Like a Second Babylon, the city—
not content with touching God—provokes
Him, teases Him with all 900 feet
of glass and girder, sin, and Sky Jump screams.
Tourists flock to test their mettle, snap
a pic or two before the leap, then run
inside and lay a twenty down on red
as if their string of luck will never end.
Far below, the Valley spreads itself
in jigsaw-puzzle pieces; to the west,
the gated palms and pools of Summerlin
mock eastern Whitney's stark blue-collar vista.
As distant peaks rise in disdainful gaze,
the lone Mojave sands stretch far away.

—Matt Forrest Esenwine

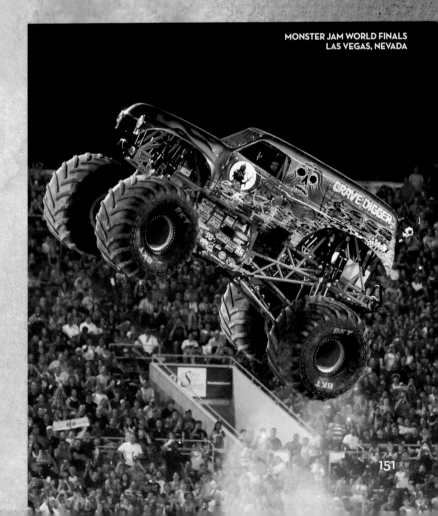

MONSTER JAM WORLD FINALS
LAS VEGAS, NEVADA

151

PACIFIC COAST

New Baby Luau

Mama Leilani is having a luau
to honor the birth of her grandbaby, Dan.
Wind off the water whispers *"Aloha"*
while torches burn brightly down on the sand.

I make a coconut toy for the baby,
Auntie makes poi–and pineapple cakes!
All of the neighbors are singing the old songs.
Down in the imu the fresh salmon bakes.

He ho ʻoheno ke ʻike aku . . .
After the feast Papa plays his guitar.
Ke kai moana nui la . . .
Everyone singing beneath the stars.

Next comes the *Ho ʻola ʻa*—the blessing—
last comes honey—so Dan will be sweet.
We lick our fingers. The moon looks down.
And we sway our way home along the beach.

—Julie Larios

Coconut Baseball

They play a strange game in Hawaii,
Called Coconut Baseball, i.e.
  You put on a lei,
   Climb a palm tree to play
And throw runners out from the skaii.

—Robert Donaldson

Eréndiro Cruz Pérez

How pretty the sunrise of the valley
While the sun of the little morning comes up
I started to whistle, to sing. Orange sun, reminds me of the oranges
We cut in the fields, I remember my family, I remember my country,
El Salvador

We pick white onions, red onions, yellow onions
How delicious are onions, but they are so heavy
Little radishes shining in my hands, I kneel to pick up from the earth
I think of the eyes of my children, four girls and two boys
and such a wonderful woman

Under the shadow of a lemon tree I hear the birds singing
The sky is a little blue piece
It reminds me of the lagoons of my homeland
By the furrows of corn

There is a worm on top of a rock
It reminds me of the worms of Fresno, Monterey, Kern, Tulare,
o de Ventura
Also of the beast, the train I travel whistling through Mexico

—Jorge Argueta

SAN ANDREAS FAULT, CALIFORNIA

Eréndiro Cruz Pérez

Que bonito el amancer del valle
Mientras va saliendo el sol de la mañanita
Me pongo a silvar, a cantar. Sol naranja de las que cortamos
En los campos, recuerdo a mi familia, recuerdo mi país, El Salvador

Cebolla que pizcamos, blanca, colorada, amarilla
Ayyyy que sabrosa, pero como pesa
Rabanito que se en enciende en mis manos de rodillas te saco de la tierra
Pienso en los ojitos de mis hijos, cuatro vichas y dos vichos y una mujer bien tallada

Bajo la sombra de un limonero escucho los pájaros cantar
El cielo es un pedacito azul,
Se parece a las lagunitas de mi tierra
Por los zurcos donde crece el maíz

Hay un gusanito trepado en una piedra
Me recuerdan a los gusanos de
Fresno, Monterey, Kern, Tulare, o de Ventura
y al tren la bestia que me trajo silvando por todo México

—Translated by Jorge Argueta

Who?

Who dumped the soup bowls on the floor?
Who shook the roof and slammed the door?

Who got the water mains to spout?
Who made the kitchen lights go out?

Who knocked down books and cracked the wall?
Who made the corner streetlight fall?

Who sent birds wheeling from their nests
and drove the kids beneath their desks?

Who quivered the river? Who made the cars
   shiver?
Who shuddered the shutters and made the hills
   mutter?

WHO DID ALL THIS?

Andreas yells, "It's not my fault!"

But it is!

—Kate Coombs

Traffic Jam, Los Angeles

We are not going where we're going.
We are not going anywhere.
Nothing moving. Nothing flowing.
Sun is shining. Tempers flare.
No back. No forth. No to and froing.
Three gardeners in a pickup stare
Straight ahead. They dream they're mowing
Their own green lawns. They do not care
That they're not going where they're going.
They are not going anywhere.
The lawyer in his Lexus knowing
He'll be late for that affair.
The actress in the back seat showing
Signs of age. She combs her hair.
No rain falling. No wind blowing.
Nothing shifts. But in the air
There wheels a blackbird, hear him crowing.
He knows our lot's beyond repair.
We are not going where we're going.
We are not going anywhere.

—David Elliott

Babel in the West

Their tower failed abuilding. Having lost
Their single tongue, the artisans moved on
To become the peoples of the world.

Filling all corners, north, south, east, and west,
They raised great cities and resplendent states,
Towers, too, but none with that great purpose.

Having become whoever they were,
Wherever they were, Chinese, Armenians,
Ethiopians, and Thais, Japanese,

And Koreans, drawn for fresh reasons
To a new honeypot with an enclave
For each of them, whether Bangladeshi,

Mexican, Filipino, Persian, Vietnamese,
They brought their two hundred plus languages
To raise the polyglot empire of

Los Angeles in Southern California,
A new hoped-for heaven for them all.

—L. M. Lewis

Hawk's Shadow

As I watched, Hawk's shadow swept
boneless dark across my feet,
then, scaled these rocky cliffs—
a silhouette, silent, fleet.

Then it thinned, grew pinpoint small
as Hawk sailed higher and higher
above the mountain wall.

I watched closely (or so I thought)
yet somehow missed that moment
when Hawk's shadow finally caught

its circling, wide-winged owner,
and those two distant loners
soared into the sun,
fused, and emerged as one.

—Kristine O'Connell George

San Francisco Pride Parade

June twenty eight—a special date
whose history we commemorate.

Whomever we love, however we dress,
all of us should feel free to express

ourselves with our own personality,
yet still feel part of the community.

Throngs come out in support to celebrate.
Just one protester this year, with slogans of hate.

Some folks react with boos and hisses,
but more respond with camp and kisses.

Around us there is joy and jubilation,
laughter, prancing, songs, flirtation.

I asked, "Why do we stand here on the side?"
My family and I march with pride.

—Lawrence Schimel

162

Golden Gate Bridge

Rising above
        the fog,
I am an aria
        of orange,
a symphony
        of steel—
a remembered
        melody.
Beneath,

I span the
Golden Gate Strait,
        from shore to
shore, with a
        chorus of cars.
What song will you
        discover
on the other side?

—*Joan Bransfield Graham*

San Francisco Fog

This stuff didn't arrive on little cat feet,
all dainty soft and silent.

It rolled in
on an ice queen's tongue—

this scrim of frost
on a wintry pane in June.

—*Sonya Sones*

163

Question for Redwood

Giant Redwood,
high-rise of the forest,
if one night, I scaled your trunk,
    climbed your limb ladder
        higher . . .
           higher . . .
                all the way to the top,
would I be up so far
    I could hitch a ride home
on a falling star?

           —Ann Whitford Paul

A Promise
to California

Also to the great Pastoral Plains, and for Oregon:
Sojourning east a while longer, soon I travel toward you, to remain,
to teach robust American love;
For I know very well that I and robust love belong among you, inland,
and along the Western Sea;
For These States tend inland, and toward the Western Sea—and I
will also.

           —Walt Whitman

Here Lies You Bet,
California

The Gold Rush, 1849

I wanted to stay when they called the earth bare
though the brambles bent high and gold filled the air.
There was gold all around, but it wasn't enough
for fortunes too dry and a frontier too tough.
Though there's gold in quick flashes of snakes in the roots
and gold in the poppies caught under our boots,
gold in the fur of the rich bears that drank
in golden-wrought rivers, there's none in our banks.
There was gold all around, but none we could spend;
the fields full of wealth but the mines a dead end.
So we hitched up our horses and faded away,
deserted our town though I wanted to stay.
The land called to wait but we bid it goodbye,
choosing gold in our hands over gold in the sky.

—*P. Maxwell Towler*

HUMBOLDT REDWOODS STATE PARK
NORTHERN CALIFORNIA

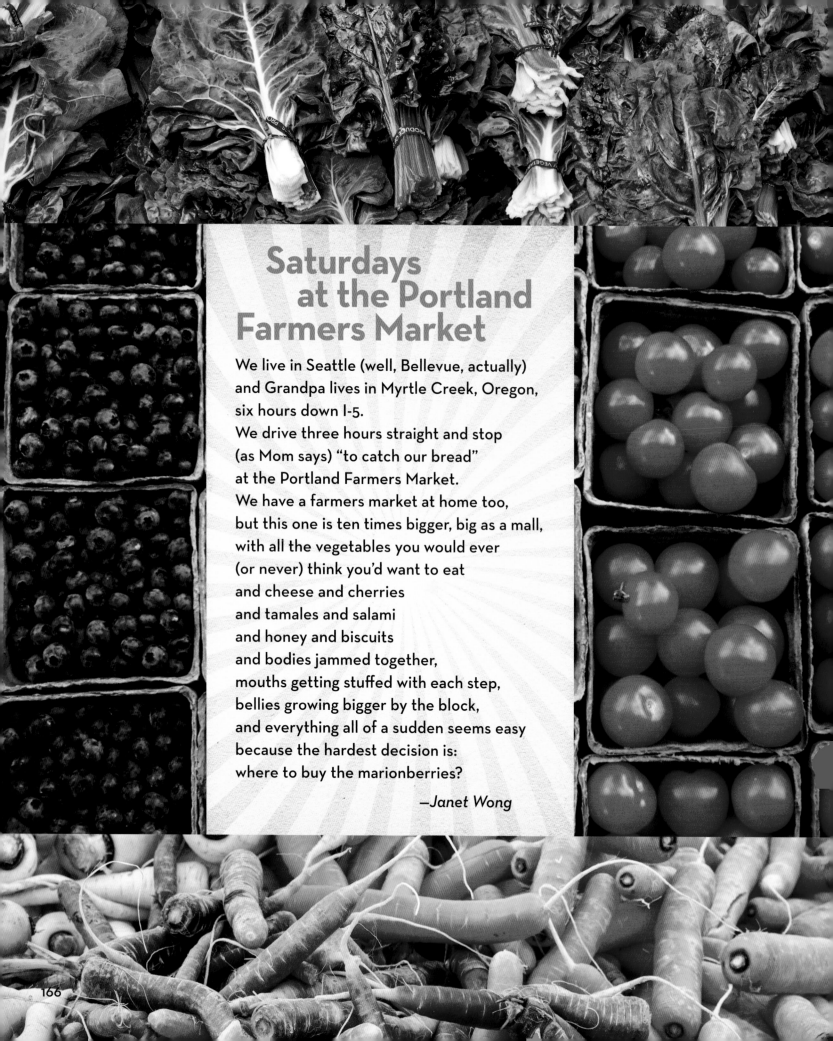

Saturdays at the Portland Farmers Market

We live in Seattle (well, Bellevue, actually)
and Grandpa lives in Myrtle Creek, Oregon,
six hours down I-5.
We drive three hours straight and stop
(as Mom says) "to catch our bread"
at the Portland Farmers Market.
We have a farmers market at home too,
but this one is ten times bigger, big as a mall,
with all the vegetables you would ever
(or never) think you'd want to eat
and cheese and cherries
and tamales and salami
and honey and biscuits
and bodies jammed together,
mouths getting stuffed with each step,
bellies growing bigger by the block,
and everything all of a sudden seems easy
because the hardest decision is:
where to buy the marionberries?

—Janet Wong

Bird Month

*The bird names mean goose, duck, and swan
in Dinak'i, the Upper Kuskokwim Athabascan
language.*

Now we see and hear daily
what the empty winter skies
were ready to receive.
Dolmoya, Tugaga', Tomo. Their cries
lift our eyes. Their necks
stretch forward, wings
push air towards us. We breathe
the end of snow.
That quiet glow of sun on the horizon
which held us close, lifts
higher and wider each day. We watch,
knowing the river
will break and flow.

—Helen Frost

Near Klamath

We stand around the burning oil drum
And we warm ourselves, our hands
And faces, in pure lapping heat.

We raise steaming cups of coffee
To our lips and we drink it
With both hands. But we are salmon

Fishermen. And now we stamp our feet
On the snow and the rocks and move upstream,
Slowly, full of love, toward the still ponds.

— Raymond Carver

Bear Country

The Savonoski Loop is a 90-mile wilderness canoe trip in Katmai National Park, Alaska.

No roads. The floatplane dropped to Naknek Lake
and left us there with boats and gear. Brown bears
big as cars patrolled the beach. They had no need
to watch us paddle off. Their noses knew.

Don't look one in the eye, the ranger said.
*Don't eat where you will sleep. And wear a bell
and shout:* Hey bear! Hey bear! *when in the woods.*
We pitched our tents in midnight dusk and woke

to spot fresh tracks the size of supper plates
along the shore. Down the north arm of Naknek
we found the portage to Grov Lake. While we
hauled boats, a bear prowled in and clawed our packs

to shreds for food. From there, we had to fish to eat,
but they could smell that too! We barely slept.
We paddled hard against a williwaw
until the Savonoski River loomed—

a foaming mess of floating trees, with feeding bears
along both banks the long twelve miles to Iliuk.
The ranger warned about this stretch: *Don't stop.
Keep space. Make noise. You can't sneak by a bear.*

—James Haines

Mount Rainier

A mountain can be graceful,
delicate, sloped like a sigh—
I've seen mountains that are shy.

I've seen mountains that don't know
they're mountains, sweet song-singing,
soft and bird-like, sky-winging.

But my mountain is bear-strong,
thick-shouldered Mt. Rainier, bull
mountain, blue-ox mountain, full

of snorts and grunts and growls,
ram-horned, beast-brave, time-tested
Rainier: wolf-howl, snow-chested.

—Julie Larios

Washington of the West

At the river riffle,
They arrive:
White-coiffed forefathers,
Dignified and wise,
A fierce gleam in yellow eyes.
On branch and beach
They assemble:
Perched to hone bills,
Ruffle feathers,
And offer fishy critiques
In a colloquy of squeaks.
Congress in session.

—Lee Wardlaw

Frozen **Town**

Barrow, Alaska
The Northernmost City in the United States

A rumble of trucks outside our window,
a swooshing of sleds, a chattering of voices
calling house to house in the semi-dark of day;
a world wrapped halfway in Arctic Ocean.

Outside is the deep freeze of caribou and ice traps,
blizzards and blue turf, a city glazed in chill and shades of night.
But still, we spot fishing boats and football,
whale bones and shippers, workers and watchmen
                  and sometimes,
                    sometimes light.

—*Rebecca Kai Dotlich*

Unfrozen

Where once was...
is nowhere now.

The river has stolen
the melting land
beneath their homes.
The sea inches
closer and only
the wooden planks
of floating sidewalks
keep them from joining
the ocean's swells.

Swollen steams
revise and then
erase the shorelines.

Snowflakes light
on the urgent currents
and vanish as if
they, too, were a people
intent only
upon survival—
briefly alive
in the heat of the moment.

—*Michael J. Rosen*

NEARLY ALL NATIVE ALASKAN VILLAGES ARE BUILT ON THE COAST OF THE GULF OF ALASKA OR THE BERING,
CHUKCHI, OR BEAUFORT SEAS. IN SOME AREAS, SUCH AS THE NEWTOK VILLAGE WHERE YUPIK ESKIMOS HAVE
SUBSISTED FOR CENTURIES, FLOODS CAUSED BY GLOBAL WARMING ERODE AS MUCH AS 300 FEET (91 M) OF
SHORELINE EACH YEAR. THE YUPIK ARE CONSIDERED THE FIRST REFUGEES OF GRADUAL CLIMATE CHANGE.

CHILDREN · OF · A · COMMON · MOTHER

The Peace Arch
Between the
US and Canada

South and North like to venture forth
  And cross our friendly border.
We share so much and keep in touch.
  Welcomes are always in order.

It's not just weather we share together,
  It's language, geography, song,
Sports, TV, our democracy,
  The list is wonderfully long . . .

Side by side good neighbors abide
  But on this we disagree:
Canadians are wed to the letter Zed
  While Americans love their Zee.

—*Avis Harley*

BUILT BETWEEN BLAINE, WASHINGTON, AND SURREY, BRITISH
COLUMBIA, CANADA, THE PEACE ARCH SYMBOLIZES A LONG
HISTORY OF PEACE BETWEEN THE UNITED STATES AND CANADA.

Belle Benchley

1882–1972

I was the bookkeeper, that's all.
At noon I'd watch the zebras loll.
I'd study wombats eating lunch
I really did not know that much
about the zoo.

I saw the llama wasn't well—
how did I know? It's hard to tell.
I pointed out a listless gnu
(for I read volumes about zoos.)

Some people swore our chief was rude—
depends upon your point of view.
(Recall he built this cageless place
which opened 1922).

It may be Dr. Wegeforth's rage
that drove three zoo leaders away.
He marched to my desk, bent down and said:
"You try and run it—go ahead."

And so I did.

—*April Halprin Wayland*

Pacific Coast

Sacajawea

1788–1812

We name rivers and mountains in her honor.
We celebrate her life with statues and a stamp.
A life that was never her own.

Kidnapped as a child.
Taken far from home.
Sold to a fur trader.

A mother at fifteen.

"Hired" at no pay on the grand expedition.
She was interpreter, guide, and symbol
of peace.

Facing the same hunger and exhaustion as the men.
A thousand-mile walk to the Pacific.
With her baby on her back.
With her baby on her back.
With her baby on her back.

—*Deborah Ruddell*

TERRI

TORIES

Problems with Hurricanes

A campesino looked at the air
And told me:
With hurricanes it's not the wind
or the noise or the water.
I'll tell you he said:
it's the mangoes, avocados
green plantains and bananas
flying into town like projectiles.
How would your family
feel if they had to tell
the generations that you
got killed by a flying
banana.
Death by drowning has honor
If the wind picked you up
and slammed you
against a mountain boulder
this would not carry shame
but
to suffer a mango smashing
your skull or a plantain hitting your
temple at 70 miles per hour
is the ultimate disgrace.
The campesino takes off his hat—
as a sign of respect
toward the fury of the wind
And says:
Don't worry about the noise
Don't worry about the water
Don't worry about the wind—
If you are going out
beware of mangoes
and all such beautiful
sweet things.

—*Victor Hernández Cruz*

Old World
New World

Spices and gold once cast a spell
on bearded men in caravels.

New World New World cried history
Old World Old World sighed every tree.

But Indian tribes long, long ago
had sailed this archipelago.

They who were used to flutes of bone
translated talk of wind on stone.

Yet their feathered tongues were drowned
when Discovery beat its drum.

New World New World—spices and gold
Old World Old World—the legends told.

New World New World—cried history
Old World Old World—sighed every tree.

—*John Agard*

Guam

Is "Where America's Day Begins."
Is the "westernmost furthest forward
    sovereign US territory in the Pacific."
Is a non-self-governing colony.
Is a US citizen ever since the 1950 Organic Act . . . .
Is a duty-free port outside the US Customs Zone.
Is expected to homeport the Pacific fleet.
Is an acronym for "Give Us American Military. . . ."
Is a target.
Is America's front porch to Asia.
Is a mini-Hawai'i.
Is strategically invisible. . . .
Is a beach for sunburnt tourists in bikinis.
Is an acronym for "Give Us Asian Money."
Is air-conditioned.
Is updating its Facebook status.
Is a punchline in Hollywood movie jokes. . . .
Is learning English as a Colonial Language (ECL).
Is frequent flyer miles.
Is endangered.
Is one of [our] most curious possessions.
Is no longer Guam.

—*Craig Santos Perez*

Winnowing

(Escogiendo habichuelas)

Mama would say
"If they float throw them out.
Esas no sirven"
Somehow it made me sad.
I didn't know if I should keep
the half-gnawed beans.
I found gray pebbles,
stowaway peas,
tiny chips of wood.
"Just like life"
Mama would say
I separated good from the bad
winnowing granma's bowl of beans
at the kitchen table
the cool beans ran through my fingers
and into my heart.

—*Judy Vasquez*

LAST THOUGHTS

You're a Grand Old Flag

You're a grand old flag,
You're a high flying flag
And forever in peace may you wave.
You're the emblem of
The land I love.
The home of the free and the brave.
Ev'ry heart beats true
'neath the Red, White and Blue,
Where there's never a boast or brag.
Should auld acquaintance be forgot,
Keep your eye on the grand old flag.

—George M. Cohan

From *Let America* **Be America Again**

Let America be America again.
Let it be the dream it used to be.
Let it be the pioneer on the plain
Seeking a home where he himself is free.

(America never was America to me.)

Let America be the dream the dreamers dreamed—
Let it be that great strong land of love
Where never kings connive nor tyrants scheme
That any man be crushed by one above.

(It never was America to me.)

O, let my land be a land where Liberty
Is crowned with no false patriotic wreath,
But opportunity is real, and life is free,
Equality is in the air we breathe.

(There's never been equality for me,
Nor freedom in this "homeland of the free.")

—Langston Hughes

I Am More

I am more than the sum of my parts.
I am more. I am more. I am more.

I am...

Colorful, a kaleidoscope of human faces.
Immense, a wonderland of magical places.

Surprising, stereotype blown wide open.
Brave: bruised and beaten but never broken.

Daring... to build the future, one lemonade stand at a time.
Ambitious: there is no ladder, no mountain I won't climb.

I am America, one-word confetti.
When you look what do you see?
I am more than the sum of my parts.
I am more. I am more. I am more.

I am...

Exciting, a flashmob at Grand Central Station
Wild, an untamed, unruly nation.

Loud, when I whisper my name, I shout.
Wounded, they can count me down but never out.

Magnificent as a million women marching through the street.
Free, skipping through the sprinkler in boiling August heat.

I am America, one-word confetti.
My country, 'tis of thee.
I am more than the sum of my parts.
I am more.
I am more.
I am more.

I am the idea of an idea, all that is or may ever be.
I am more.
I am the best of my ancestors, elevating me.
I am more.
I am...
ColorfulImmenseSurprisingBraveDaringAmbitiousExcitingWildLoudWoundedMagnificentFree
I am more.

I am you
and you
and you . . . .

I am America, one-word confetti.
Can you see the possibility?
I am more than the sum of my parts.
I am more.
I am more.
I am more.

—Leigh Lewis

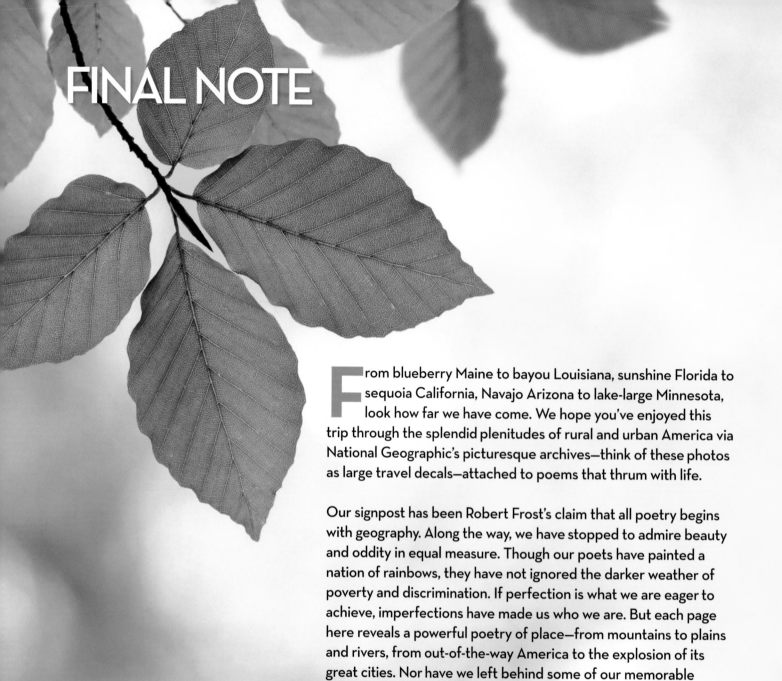

FINAL NOTE

From blueberry Maine to bayou Louisiana, sunshine Florida to sequoia California, Navajo Arizona to lake-large Minnesota, look how far we have come. We hope you've enjoyed this trip through the splendid plenitudes of rural and urban America via National Geographic's picturesque archives—think of these photos as large travel decals—attached to poems that thrum with life.

Our signpost has been Robert Frost's claim that all poetry begins with geography. Along the way, we have stopped to admire beauty and oddity in equal measure. Though our poets have painted a nation of rainbows, they have not ignored the darker weather of poverty and discrimination. If perfection is what we are eager to achieve, imperfections have made us who we are. But each page here reveals a powerful poetry of place—from mountains to plains and rivers, from out-of-the-way America to the explosion of its great cities. Nor have we left behind some of our memorable citizens whose lives have enriched us all.

Have we omitted anything? In a nation as vast as the United States, of course we have. And so we invite you, dear reader, to think back to a family visit when you saw or heard something uniquely American, and write a poem to mark the occasion. Or perhaps your subject lies just around the corner? Use any poetic form that appeals to you. You're certain to have as much fun as the poets in these pages have had in recognizing their homeland.

—*J. Patrick Lewis*

Here is a selected bibliography of children's books on wordplay in poetry that you might find especially useful as you explore your own paths to poetry.

ACROSTICS

Harley, Avis. *African Acrostics: A Word in Edgeways.* Candlewick, 2009.

Schnur, Steven. *Autumn: An Alphabet Acrostic.* Clarion, 1997. (See also his Winter, Spring, and Summer acrostic books in this series.)

ANAGRAMS

Lederer, Richard. *The Circus of Words.* Chicago Review Press, 2001.

Raczka, Bob. *Lemonade: and Other Poems Squeezed From a Single Word.* Roaring Brook, 2011.

DOUBLE DACTYLS, OR IF YOU PREFER, HIGGLEDY-PIGGLEDYS

Hecht, Anthony, and John Hollander, eds. *Jiggery Pokery: A Compendium of Double Dactyls.* Atheneum, 1967.

EPITAPHS

Lewis, J. Patrick. *Once Upon a Tomb: Gravely Humorous Verses.* Candlewick, 2006.

Lewis, J. Patrick, and Jane Yolen. *Last Laughs: Animal Epitaphs.* Charlesbridge, 2012.

Yolen, Jane, and J. Patrick Lewis. *Last Laughs: Prehistoric Epitaphs.* Charlesbridge, 2017.

HAIKU

Farrar, Sid. *The Year Comes Round: Haiku Through the Seasons.* Albert Whitman, 2012.

George, Kristine O'Connell. *Fold Me a Poem.* Houghton Mifflin Harcourt, 2005.

Issa, Kobayashi. *Today and Today.* Scholastic, 2007.

Mora, Pat. *Yum! Mmm! Qué Rico! Americas' Sproutings.* Lee & Low, 2007.

Prelutsky, Jack. *If Not for the Cat: Haiku.* Greenwillow, 2004.

Raczka, Bob. *Guyku: A Year of Haiku for Boys.* Houghton Mifflin Harcourt, 2010.

Rosen, Michael J. *The Cuckoo's Haiku and Other Birding Poems.* Candlewick, 2009.

——. *The Hound Dog's Haiku and Other Poems for Dog Lovers.* Candlewick, 2011.

Snyder, Betsy. *I Haiku You.* Random House, 2012.

Wardlaw, Lee. *Won Ton: A Cat Tale Told in Haiku.* Henry Holt, 2011.

Yolen, Jane. *Least Things: Poems About Small Natures.* Wordsong/Boyds Mills, 2003.

Ziefert, Harriet. *Hanukkah Haiku.* Blue Apple Books, 2008.

LIPOGRAMS

Lawson, JonArno. *A Voweller's Bestiary.* Porcupine's Quill, 2008.

LITTLE WILLIES

Invented by Harry Graham, showcased by X. J. Kennedy in his Brats books.

PALINDROMES

Agee, Jon. *Go, Hang a Salami! I'm a Lasagna Hog! And Other Palindromes.* Farrar, Straus, Giroux, 1994. (See also the other books in this series.)

PARODIES

Levine, Gail Carson. *Forgive Me, I Meant to Do It: False Apology Poems.* HarperCollins, 2012.

Shapiro, Karen Jo. *I Must Go Down to the Beach Again.* Charlesbridge, 2007.

Sidman, Joyce. *This Is Just to Say: Poems of Apology and Forgiveness.* Houghton Mifflin Harcourt, 2007.

PORTMANTEAUS

Prelutsky, Jack. *Scranimals.* HarperCollins, 2002.

——. *Behold the Bold Umbrellaphant.* Greenwillow, 2006.

——. *Stardines Swim High Across the Sky.* Greenwillow, 2013.

INDEX

TITLE INDEX

POET INDEX

FIRST LINE INDEX

INDEX

INDEX

SUBJECT INDEX

Boldface indicates illustrations.

A

Airports 95
Alabama 64-65, **64-65**
Alaska 170-171, **170-171**
Albuquerque, New Mexico 147
Aldrin, Edwin F. "Buzz," Jr. 132
Alligators 80, **80-81**
American ideals 6, 11, **11**, 13, 39, **39**, 180-182
American Revolution 10, 29
Amish 49, **49**
Appalachian Trail 16, **16-17**
April Fool's Day 118
Armstrong, Neil A. 132, **132-133**
Aviation 95, 125, **125**

B

Babies 154
Bald eagles 8, **8-9**, 169, **169**
Barrow, Alaska 170
Baseball **118-119**, 119, 155
Basketball 67, **67**
Beaches 27, **27**, 50-51, **50-51**, **180-181**
Bears 168, **168**
Biltmore House, Asheville, North Carolina 69, **69**
Birmingham, Alabama 64, **64**
Black Hills, South Dakota 115, **115**
Blue Ridge Mountains 60, **60-61**
Blueberries 21, **21**
Boats 31, **31**
Bonneville Salt Flats, Utah 150, **150**
Bookmobiles 97, **97**
Boston, Massachusetts 24-25, **24-25**
Boudreau, Earlene 75
Bridges 163, **163**
Brookings, South Dakota 111
Brown bears 168, **168**
Buffalo 121, **121**

C

California 156-165, **156-165**
Canoes 93, **93**
Cars 89, **89**, 113, 158, **158**
Caves 61, **61**
Cawker City, Kansas 124
Chandrasekhar, Subrahmanyan 133
Cherry blossoms 56, **56-57**
Chicago, Illinois 94-95, **94-95**
Christmas cards 23
Civil rights 54, **54**, 78-79, **78-79**
Civil War 48
Clay artists 131, **131**
Climate change 171
Clotheslines 90, **90**
Coleman, Bessie 125, **125**
Colorado River 146, **146**
Continental Divide 139
Cowboys 137, **137**

D

Disney World, Orlando, Florida 83
Dog shows 47, **47**
Drive-in movies 129, **129**
Dust Bowl 120, **120**

E

Eagles 8, **8-9**, 169, **169**
Earhart, Amelia 125, **125**
Earthquakes 157
El Paso, Texas 126-127, **126-127**
Ellis Island, New York 36, **36**

F

Fair Play, Missouri 87
Farms
    Great Plains 116-117, 117, 127, **127**
    New England 20-21, **20-21**
    Pacific Coast 156-157, **156-157**, 166, **166**
    Rocky Mountain West 136, **136**
Fayetteville, Arkansas 72
Festivals 44, 86, 96, **96**, 147, **147**, 161, **161**
Field, Eugene 106
Fishing 146, **146**
Fitzgerald, Ella 76, **76**
Fog 163, **163**
Food
    Mid-Atlantic 42-43, **42-43**
    Midwest 91, **91**, 102, **102**
    New England 20-22, 25
    Pacific Coast 161, **161**, 166, **166**
    Rocky Mountain West 142-143, **142-143**
    Territories 176, **176**, 179, **179**
Fourth of July 26, **26**, 118, **182-183**
Foxtails 81
Friendship 19, **19**

G

Garlic 161, **161**
Gay pride 30, 162, **162**
Georgia 71
Gettysburg, Battle of (1863) 48
Gilroy Garlic Festival, California 161, **161**
Global warming 171
Gold rush 165
Golden Gate Bridge, San Francisco, California 163, **163**
Great Lakes 92, **92-93**
Groundhog's Day 47, **47**
Guam 179

H

Halloween 68
Hanukkah 99
Hawaii 154-155, **154-155**
Hawks 159, **159**
Hmong 160, **160**
Holiday, Billie "Lady Day" 38, **38**
Holidays 22; see also specific holidays
Holland, Michigan 96, **96**
Homelessness 100-101
Hot air balloons 147, **147**
Hudson River, New York 44
Hurricanes 75, 178

I

Ice skating 98, **98**
Immigration
    Mid-Atlantic 34, 36-37, **36-37**
    Midwest 103
    Pacific Coast 156-157, 158, 160, **160**
    Southeast 82, **82**
Independence Day 26, **26**, 118, **182-183**
Indiana Dunes 91, **91**
Indianapolis 500 89, **89**

J

Jackalopes 138

K

Kansas 122-123, **122-123**
Keller, Helen 70, **70**
Kennedy, John F. 130
Kentucky Derby 66, **66**
King, Martin Luther, Jr. 54, **54**
Knishes 43, **43**
Kudzu 65, **65**

L

Ladora, Iowa 87
Las Vegas, Nevada 151, **151**
Lincoln, Abraham 54-55, **54-55**, 114, **114**
Little Bighorn, Montana 148
Los Angeles, California 158, **158**
Louisiana 74-75, **74-75**
Love 30, **30**

M

Mammoth Cave, Kentucky 61, **61**
Marriage 30, 82, **82**, 92
Martin, Trayvon 79
Menorahs 99
Mississippi River 104-105, **104-105**
Monster trucks 151, **151**
Montana State Fair 136, **136**
Moon landing 132, **132-133**
Mountains 60, **60-61**, 169, **169**
Movies 128, **128**, 129, **129**
Murals 52, **52**

N

Native Americans 140, 148, 149, **149**, 173, **173**
Nebraska 113
Nelson, Willie 88
New Hampshire 17
New Orleans, Louisiana 75
New Year's Eve 26, 41, **41**
New York City 34-41, **34-41**
Niagara Falls **44-45**, 45
North Dakota 110-111, **110-111**

O

Omaha, Nebraska 116-117, 117
Owens, Jesse 77, **77**

P

Passover 22, **22**
Peace Arch, Canada-U.S.A. 172, **172**
Philadelphia, Pennsylvania 42, **42**, 52, **52**
Pie Town, New Mexico 143
Pigs 136, **136**
Portland Farmers Market, Oregon 166, **166**
Poverty 100-101
Presley, Elvis 62, **62**

Q

Quahogs 21, **21**

R

Rafting 146, **146**
Rainier, Mount, Washington 169, **169**
The Ramones 88
Redwood trees 164, **164-165**
Revolutionary War 10, 29

Rodeos 137, **137**
Roosevelt, Teddy 114, **114**, 121
Roses 8-9, 9
Rushmore, Mount, South Dakota 114, **114**

S

Sacajawea 173, **173**
Salmon 167, **167**
San Francisco, California 162-163, **162-163**
School buses 124, **124**
Seashells 177, **177**
Seasons 17
Seeger, Pete 44
September 11, 2001 35
Soap Box Derby 89
Sonoran Desert 141
Space exploration 132-133, **132-133**
Spelling bees 46, **46**
Spring 17
St. Patrick's Day 95, **95**
Statue of Liberty, New York Harbor 34, **34-35**
Stearns County Bookmobile, Minnesota 97, **97**
Stratosphere, Las Vegas, Nevada 151, **151**
Suburbia 106, **106-107**
Swamps **70-71**, 71
Sweat lodges 140

T

Thanksgiving 23, 143
Till, Emmett 78
Traffic jams 158, **158**
Trees 164, **164-165**
Trussville, Alabama 76
Tulips 96, **96**
Turkey buzzards 86, **86**
Twain, Mark 105, **105**, 106
Twine 124, **124**
Twinsburg Festival, Ohio 96, **96**
Typo, Kentucky 72

U

Underground Railroad 56

V

Valentine's Day 30
Vermont 17
Voting rights 39, **39**

W

Washington, George 29, 114, **114**
Wayne, John 128, **128**
Weddings 30, 82, **82**, 92
Whales 18, **18-19**
White House, Washington, D.C. 54-55, 55
White-water rafting 146, **146**
Women's rights 39, **39**

Y

Yellowstone National Park 138-139, 139

Z

Zoos 173

189

TEXT & PHOTO CREDITS

6. **America the Beautiful.** Katharine Lee Bates.
8. **Naming the American Eagle.** Steven Withrow. Copyright © Steven Withrow. Reprinted with permission of the author.
9. **Our Rose.** Joyce Sidman. Copyright © Joyce Sidman. Reprinted with permission of the author.
10. **The Gift Outright.** Robert Frost.
11. **Power to the People.** Carole Boston Weatherford. Copyright © Carole Boston Weatherford. Reprinted with permission of the author.
12. **I Hear America Singing.** Walt Whitman.
13. **I, Too.** Langston Hughes. From *The Collected Poems of Langston Hughes* by Langston Hughes, edited by Arnold Rampersad with David Roessel, Associate Editor, copyright © 1994 by the Estate of Langston Hughes. Used by permission of Alfred A. Knopf, an imprint of the Knopf Doubleday Publishing Group, a division of Penguin Random House LLC. All rights reserved.

NEW ENGLAND
16. **A Note from the Trail.** Amy Ludwig VanDerwater. Copyright © 2017 by Amy Ludwig VanDerwater. Reprinted by permission of Curtis Brown, Ltd.
17. **Spring in New Hampshire.** Claude McKay.
17. **Vermont Seasons.** X. J. Kennedy. Copyright © X. J. Kennedy. Reprinted with permission of the author.
18. **Whale Watch, Cape Cod.** Steven Withrow. Copyright © Steven Withrow. Reprinted with permission of the author.
19. **Friendship Circle—7:30 AM.** Richard Michelson. Copyright © Richard Michelson. Reprinted with permission of the author.
20. **The Man Who Scattered Pollen Underneath the Sun.** Michele Krueger. Copyright © Michele Krueger. Reprinted with permission of the author.
20. **Roadside Stand.** Marilyn Singer. Copyright © Marilyn Singer. Reprinted with permission of the author.
21. **Blueberry Barrens.** Ralph Fletcher. Copyright © Ralph Fletcher. Reprinted with permission of the author.
21. **Sing Hey-Ho for Quahogs!** Leslie Bulion. Copyright © Leslie Bulion. Reprinted with permission of the author.
22. **The Last Passover.** Liz Rosenberg. Copyright © Liz Rosenberg. Reprinted with permission of the author.
22. **Holidays.** Henry Wadsworth Longfellow.
23. **If I Had Nothing Else to Do, I'd Write A Christmas Card to You.** Mariel Bede. Copyright © Mariel Bede. Reprinted with permission of the author.
23. **The Menu at the First Thanksgiving, 1621.** John Bucholz. Copyright © John Bucholz. Reprinted with permission of the author.
24. **Boston.** Edwin Arlington Robinson.
24. **At Boston Public Garden, Summer.** Steven Withrow. Copyright © Steven Withrow. Reprinted with permission of the author.
25. **Boston Marathon.** Kate Coombs. Copyright © Kate Coombs. Reprinted with permission of the author.
25. **Boston Baked Beans: A Recipe.** David Elliott. Copyright © David Elliott. Reprinted with permission of the author.
26. **Independence Day.** Leslie Bulion. Copyright © Leslie Bulion. Reprinted with permission of the author.
26. **Watching the New Year's Eve Party Through the Staircase.** J. Patrick Lewis. Copyright © J. Patrick Lewis. Reprinted with permission of the author.
27. **Beach Days.** Joyce Sidman. Copyright © Joyce Sidman. Reprinted with permission of the author.
28. **In Frost Country.** Rhina P. Espaillat. Copyright © Rhina P. Espaillat. Reprinted with permission of the author.
28. **Upstairs in Amherst.** Rhina P. Espaillat. Copyright © Rhina P. Espaillat. Reprinted with permission of the author.
28. **Yawp.** Rhina P. Espaillat. Copyright © Rhina P. Espaillat. Reprinted with permission of the author.
29. **The Continental Army.** Marilyn Nelson. Copyright © Marilyn Nelson. Reprinted with permission of the author.
30. **To Have and To Hold.** Lesléa Newman. Copyright © 2017 by Lesléa Newman. Reprinted by permission of Curtis Brown, Ltd.
30. **Valentine.** Donald Hall. Copyright © Donald Hall. Reprinted with permission of the author.
31. **Product.** George Oppen. Copyright © 1975 by George Oppen. Reprinted by permission of New Directions Publishing Corp.

MID-ATLANTIC
34. **The New Colossus.** Emma Lazarus.
35. **Recuerdo.** Edna St. Vincent Millay.
35. **September Twelfth, 2001.** X. J. Kennedy. *The Lords of Misrule: Poems 1992-2001.* pp. 88. © 2002 X. J. Kennedy. Reprinted with permission of Johns Hopkins University Press.
36. **Ellis Island Mathematics.** Jane Yolen. Copyright © 2017 by Jane Yolen. Reprinted by permission of Curtis Brown, Ltd.
36. **An Irish Emigrant Bound for America.** Mariel Bede. Copyright © Mariel Bede. Reprinted with permission of the author.
37. **Bringing Palestine Home to America.** Ibtisam Barakat. Copyright © Ibtisam Barakat. Reprinted with permission of the author.
38. **Lady Day.** Peggy Gifford. Copyright © Peggy Gifford. Reprinted with permission of the author.
38. **Eliza, Age 10, Harlem.** Rita Dove. From *Collected Poems 1974-2004*, W.W. Norton & Company. © 2004, 2016 by Rita Dove. Reprinted by permission of the author.
39. **Poets House.** Douglas Florian. Copyright © Douglas Florian. Reprinted with permission of the author.
39. **Triolet.** Tricia Stohr-Hunt. Copyright © Tricia Stohr-Hunt. Reprinted with permission of the author.
40. **New York Notes.** Harvey Shapiro. "New York Notes" from *How Charlie Shavers Died and Other Poems* © 2001 by Harvey Shapiro. Published by Wesleyan University Press. Used by permission.

40. **Fish Tales.** Sydell Rosenberg. Copyright © Sydell Rosenberg. Reprinted with permission of the author.
40. **High-Rise Window Washer.** Douglas Florian. Copyright © Douglas Florian. Reprinted with permission of the author.
41. **New Year's Eve: A 21st Century Ball Drop.** Bobbi Katz. "New Year's Eve: A 21st Century Ball Drop" Copyright © 2018 Bobbi Katz.
42. **Asian Market.** Linda Sue Park. Copyright © 2018 Linda Sue Park. Reprinted by permission of Curtis Brown, Ltd.
42. **Never Say No.** Laura Purdie Salas. Copyright © Laura Purdie Salas. Reprinted with permission of the author.
43. **Ode to a Knish Shop.** Lesléa Newman. Copyright © 2017 by Lesléa Newman. Reprinted by permission of Curtis Brown, Ltd.
44. **The Great Hudson River Revival.** Bobbi Katz. Copyright © 2018 Bobbi Katz.
45. **Niagara Falls.** P. Maxwell Towler. Copyright © 2018 P. Maxwell Towler. Reprinted with permission of the author.
46. **Spellbound.** Avis Harley. Copyright © Avis Harley. Reprinted with permission of the author.
47. **Groundhognostication.** B. J. Lee. Copyright © B. J. Lee. Reprinted with permission of the author.
47. **Champion Betty.** Allan Wolf. Copyright © Allan Wolf. Reprinted with permission of the author.
48. **Silent Sentinel.** Kelly Ramsdell Fineman. Copyright © Kelly Ramsdell Fineman. Reprinted with permission of the author.
49. **Kishacoquillas Valley Ride.** Ann Hostetler. Copyright © Ann Hostetler. Reprinted with permission of the author.
50. **Beach Day.** Laura Shovan. Copyright © Laura Shovan. Reprinted with permission of the author.
50. **Water, Water Everywhere: A Delaware Chant.** Laura Purdie Salas. Copyright © Laura Purdie Salas. Reprinted with permission of the author.
51. **Right Time, Right Place.** Helen Frost. Copyright © 1993 by Helen Frost. Reprinted by permission of Curtis Brown, Ltd.
52. **Mural Compass.** Robyn Hood Black. Copyright © Robyn Hood Black Reprinted with permission of the author.
52. **City of Brotherly Love.** Charles Waters. Copyright © Charles Waters. Reprinted with permission of the author.
53. **Black Boys Play the Classics.** Toi Derricotte. From *Tender*, by Toi Dericotte, © 1997. Reprinted by permission of the University of Pittsburgh Press.
53. **The Strand Theater.** Joan Bransfield Graham. Reprinted with permission of Joan Bransfield Graham, who controls the rights.
54. **Lincoln Memorial.** Charles Waters. Copyright © Charles Waters. Reprinted with permission of the author.
55. **That April Train.** Jane Yolen. Copyright © 2017 by Jane Yolen. Reprinted by permission of Curtis Brown, Ltd.
55. **The White House.** Kelly Ramsdell Fineman. Copyright © Kelly Ramsdell Fineman. Reprinted with permission of the author.
56. **The Underground Railroad.** Sara Holbrook. Copyright © Sara Holbrook. Reprinted with permission of the author.
56. **Note to Nature Regarding Cherry Blossoms.** Rebecca Kai Dotlich. Copyright © 2017 Rebecca Kai Dotlich. Reprinted by permission of Curtis Brown, Ltd.
57. **George Washington's Monument.** Sharif S. Elmusa. Copyright © Sharif S. Elmusa. Reprinted with permission of the author.

SOUTHEAST
60. **One Minute Till Sunrise.** Marc Harshman. Copyright © Marc Harshman. Reprinted with permission of the author.
60. **Blue Ridge Mountains.** Georgia Heard. Copyright © 2017 by Georgia Heard. Reprinted by permission of Curtis Brown, Ltd.
61. **Mammoth Cave National Park, Kentucky.** Steven Withrow. Copyright © Steven Withrow. Reprinted with permission of the author.
62. **Standing Outside Graceland.** Eric Ode. Copyright © Eric Ode. Reprinted with permission of the author.
63. **The Hall.** Eric Ode. Copyright © Eric Ode. Reprinted with permission of the author.
64. **Birmingham.** Charles Ghigna. Copyright © Charles Ghigna. Reprinted with permission of the author.
64. **City Home.** Amy Ludwig VanDerwater. Copyright © 2017 by Amy Ludwig VanDerwater. Reprinted by permission of Curtis Brown, Ltd.
65. **Alabama Kudzu.** Charles Ghigna. Copyright © Charles Ghigna. Reprinted with permission of the author.
65. **Daybreak in Alabama.** Langston Hughes. From *The Collected Poems of Langston Hughes* by Langston Hughes, edited by Arnold Rampersad with David Roessel, Associate Editor, copyright © 1994 by the Estate of Langston Hughes. Used by permission of Alfred A. Knopf, an imprint of the Knopf Doubleday Publishing Group, a division of Penguin Random House LLC. All rights reserved.
66. **The Derby.** Ron Koertge. Copyright © Ron Koertge. Reprinted with permission of the author.
67. **If the Court Could Speak.** Charles R. Smith Jr.. Copyright © Charles R. Smith, Jr. Reprinted with permission of the author.
67. **Nicknames in the NBA.** Anonymous.
68. **It Must Be Halloween.** Allan Wolf. Copyright © Allan Wolf. Reprinted with permission of the author.
68. **Ozark Hills.** Mary Nida Smith. Copyright © Mary Nida Smith. Reprinted with permission of the author.
69. **The Biltmore House.** Allan Wolf. Copyright © Allan Wolf. Reprinted with permission of the author.
70. **Listening.** Linda Kulp Trout. Copyright © Linda Kulp Trout. Reprinted with permission of the author.
71. **Swamp Song.** Liz Rosenberg. Copyright © Liz Rosenberg. Reprinted with permission of the author.
71. From **A Georgia Song.** Maya Angelou. "A Georgia Song" from *Shaker, Why Don't You Sing?* by Maya Angelou, copyright © 1983 by Maya Angelou. Used by permission of Random House, an imprint and division of Penguin Random House LLC, and Little, Brown Book Group Limited. All rights reserved.
72. **No Mistake.** George Ella Lyon. Copyright © George Ella Lyon. Reprinted with permission of the author.
72. **Fayetteville as in Fate.** Mohja Kahf. "Fayetteville as in Fate" from *Emails From Scheherazad* by Mohja Kahf. Gainesville: University Press of Florida, 2003, pp. 6-7. Reprinted with permission of the University Press of Florida.
73. **Grandma's Front Porch.** Eric Ode. Copyright © Eric Ode. Reprinted with permission of the author.
74. **Louisiana Bayou Song.** Margaret Simon. Copyright © Margaret Simon. Reprinted with permission of the author.
75. **The Ninth Ward.** J. Patrick Lewis. Copyright © J. Patrick Lewis. Reprinted with permission of the author.
76. **Ella.** Mariel Bede. Copyright © Mariel Bede. Reprinted with permission of the author.
76. **I Give Thanks for Trussville, Alabama.** Irene Lathem. Copyright © Irene Latham. Reprinted with permission of the author.
77. **Jesse Owens.** Charles Ghigna. Copyright © Charles Ghigna. Reprinted with permission of the author.
78. **The Innocent.** J. Patrick Lewis. Copyright © J. Patrick Lewis. Reprinted with permission of the author.
79. **For Trayvon Martin.** Reuben Jackson. Copyright © Reuben Jackson. Reprinted with permission of the author.
80. **Gator Theater.** Kenn Nesbitt. Copyright © Kenn Nesbitt. Reprinted with permission of the author.
81. **Foxtail Palm Ballet.** Lee Bennett Hopkins. Copyright © 2017 by Lee Bennett Hopkins. Reprinted by permission of Curtis Brown, Ltd.
82. **An American Wedding.** Margarita Engle. Copyright © Margarita Engle. Reprinted with permission of the author.
83. **Disney World.** Georgia Heard. Copyright © 2017 by Georgia Heard. Reprinted by permission of Curtis Brown, Ltd.

MIDWEST
86. **Turkey Buzzard Time.** Tracie Vaughn. Copyright © Tracie Vaughn. Reprinted with permission of the author.
87. **Valley View.** David L. Harrison. Copyright © David L. Harrison. Reprinted with permission of the author.
87. **Poem to Be Read at 3 A.M.** Donald Justice. "Poem to Be Read at 3 A.M." from *Collected Poems by Donald Justice*, Copyright © 2004 by Donald Justice. Used by permission of Alfred A. Knopf, an imprint of the Knopf Doubleday Publishing Group, a division of Penguin Random House LLC. All rights reserved.
88. **Willie Nelson.** Kathi Appelt. Copyright © Kathi Appelt. Reprinted with permission of Pippin Properties, Inc.
88. **Ladies and Gentleman – The Ramones.** Michael Salinger. Copyright © Michael Salinger. Reprinted with permission of the author.
89. **Recipe for the First Derby Cars.** Mary Lee Hahn. Copyright © Mary Lee Hahn. Reprinted with permission of the author.
89. **The Place of 500 Miles.** Rebecca Kai Dotlich. Copyright © 2017 Rebecca Kai Dotlich. Reprinted by permission of Curtis Brown, Ltd.
90. **Clothesline.** Diane Gilliam. Copyright © Diane Gilliam. Reprinted with permission of the author.
91. **Mt. Tom.** L. M. Lewis. Copyright © L.M. Lewis. Reprinted with permission of the author.
91. **Grandpa Mails the Sea to Ohio.** Holly Thompson. Copyright © Holly Thompson. Reprinted with permission of the author.
92. **For an Island Wedding.** John Barr. Copyright © John Barr. Reprinted with permission of the author.
92. **Great Lakes.** JonArno Lawson. Copyright © JonArno Lawson. Reprinted with permission of the author.
93. **Sacred Land.** Laura Purdie Salas. Copyright © Laura Purdie Salas. Reprinted with permission of the author.
94. **Chicago, Tell Me Who You Are.** John Barr. Copyright © John Barr. Reprinted with permission of the author.
95. **O'Hare.** Tracie Vaughn. Copyright © Tracie Vaughn. Reprinted with permission of the author.
95. **The Chicago River.** Donna Marie Merritt. Copyright © Donna Marie Merritt. Reprinted with permission of the author.
96. **At the Twinsburg Festival.** Peter Kostin. Copyright © Peter Kostin. Reprinted with permission of the author.
96. **Tulip Time Festival.** Buffy Silverman. Copyright © Buffy Silverman. Reprinted with permission of the author.
97. **Bookmobile, Stearns County, Minnesota.** Joyce Sutphen. Copyright © Joyce Sutphen. Reprinted with permission of the author.
98. **Three Girls On Skates.** Joyce Sutphen. Copyright © Joyce Sutphen. Reprinted with permission of the author.
99. **Emmylou Oberkfell: Fifth Grade Poem on America.** Dave Etter. Copyright © Dave Etter. Reprinted with permission of Spoon River Press.
99. **The Menorah.** Elizabeth Steinglass. Copyright © Elizabeth Steinglass. Reprinted with permission of the author.
100. **Turtle.** George Ella Lyon. Copyright © George Ella Lyon. Reprinted with permission of the author.
101. **The Poor.** James Hayford. From *Knee-Deep in Blazing Snow* by James Hayford. Copyright © 2005 by James Hayford and Michael McCurdy. Published by WordSong, an imprint of Boyd Mills Press. Reprinted by permission.
101. **Give-Away.** George Ella Lyon. Copyright © George Ella Lyon. Reprinted with permission of the author.
102. **Cardamom Bread Topped With Walnuts.** Susan Marie Swanson. Copyright © Susan Marie Swanson. Reprinted with permission of the author.
103. **The Arabic Numbers in America.** Ibtisam Barakat. Copyright © Ibtisam Barakat. Reprinted with permission of the author.
104. **The Mississippi River.** Arnold Adoff. Copyright © 2011 by The Arnold Adoff Revocable Living Trust. Used by permission of the author.

191

Since 1888, the National Geographic Society has funded more than 12,000 research,
exploration, and preservation projects around the world. The Society receives funds from
National Geographic Partners, LLC, funded in part by your purchase. A portion of
the proceeds from this book supports this vital work. To learn more, visit natgeo.com/info.

NATIONAL GEOGRAPHIC and Yellow Border Design are trademarks of the
National Geographic Society, used under license.

For more information, visit nationalgeographic.com, call 1-800-647-5463,
or write to the following address:

National Geographic Partners
1145 17th Street N.W.
Washington, D.C. 20036-4688 U.S.A.

Visit us online at nationalgeographic.com/books

For librarians and teachers: ngchildrensbooks.org

More for kids from National Geographic:
natgeokids.com

For information about special discounts for bulk purchases, please contact
National Geographic Books Special Sales: specialsales@natgeo.com

For rights or permissions inquiries, please contact
National Geographic Books Subsidiary Rights: bookrights@natgeo.com

Designed by Kathryn Robbins

The publisher would like to thank Paige Towler, project manager;
Lori Epstein, photo editor; Mary Joe Courchesne, permissions agent;
Sally Abbey, managing editor; Joan Gossett, production editor; Catherine
Farley, copy editor; and Anne Leongson and Gus Tello, production assistants.

Library of Congress Cataloging-in-Publication Data

Names: Lewis, J. Patrick, editor.
Title: The poetry of US / [edited] by J. Patrick Lewis.
Description: Washington, DC :
National Geographic
Kids, 2017.
Identifiers: LCCN 2017035089| ISBN 9781426331855
(hardcover) | ISBN 9781426331862 (hardcover)
Subjects: LCSH: United States--Juvenile poetry. |
National characteristics, American--Juvenile poetry.
Classification: LCC PS595.U5 P66 2017 | DDC
811.008/09282--dc23
LC record available at https://lccn.loc.gov/2017035089

Printed in China
18/PPS/1